A *Bible* STORY

T. HANS

Primix Publishing
East Brunswick Office Evolution
1 Tower Center Boulevard, Ste 1510
East Brunswick, NJ 08816
www.primixpublishing.com
Phone: 1-800-538-5788

Published by Primix Publishing: 02/10/2026

ISBN: 979-8-89194-615-6(sc)
ISBN: 979-8-89194-616-3(e)

Library of Congress Control Number: 2026902017

Translations of The Bible

A BIBLE STORY

Features of "A Bible Story"

- It all starts with Jesus… and ends with love
- Love and gospel overpower selfishness and law
- It summarizes Biblical truth in Bible words
- Five different versions of the Bible are quoted
- A general time-line is laid out to aid understanding
- Repetition and less important passages are left out
- Narrow historical perspectives are omitted
- It focuses on New Testament essentials for the 20th century
- A Christian perspective—central religious and spiritual truth
- It blends many "letters" together for today's Christians
- Similar passages are organized together to compliment one another
- "Treasured passages" are finally identified and bracketed
- Passages are interpreted generally by placement in chapters
- It offers interesting transitional reading one passage after another
- It encourages Bible reading—compact, interesting, delightful, surprising

- A resource for Bible study with special translations
- It pulls passages out of context to focus attention on "the center"
- An emphasis is on the positive in passage selection
- Favorite passages are easy to find and understand
- Motivation and inspiration—heavy "carrot" and light "stick"
- The Bible through "a prophet's" eyes
- A great witness for the kind of change Jesus came to reveal
- A resource for "new life and living"
- The organizer's "top ten" Bible passages—or pick your own
- Easy to put down and pick up for small time slots
- A good gift idea for meditation, inspiration, study and discussion

Translations:

Good News Bible—GNB
New English Bible—NEB
New International Version—NIV
Revised Standard Version—RSV
The Net Bible—NET
Thomas Hans Olson Version—HOV
(Initials follow chapter and verse)

50 Significant Passages:

Symbols follow translation abbreviations

"Top Ten" = *

"Plus Twenty" = +

"Final Twenty" = ~

References follow last chapter:

Old Testament and New Testament

Special Word Count:

Total times each word occurs in the document

Postscript: "A Dream"

PROLOGUE

Jesus taught truth and changed people's lives with his stories and parables. Thus this book—"A Bible Story"—is meant to reveal the Spirit of love… as well as reach deep into hearts and minds to foster discipleship. The intent is to inspire readers to move toward God's Kingdom on earth and "new life" now, and forever. In order to get into the mood for "A Bible Story" let me share a simple account seen recently on the internet. I think it conveys truth, evokes feelings and inspires the kind of divine creativity called forth by the Holy Spirit.

A Baby's Hug

We were the only family with children in the restaurant. I sat Erik in a highchair and noticed everyone was quietly sitting and talking. Suddenly, Erik squealed with glee and said, "Hi." He pounded his fat baby hands on the high chair tray. His eyes were crinkled in laughter and his mouth was bared in a toothless grin, as he wriggled and giggled with merriment.

I looked around and saw the source of his merriment. It was a man whose pants were baggy with a zipper at half-mast and his toes poked out of would-be shoes. His shirt was dirty and his hair was uncombed and unwashed. His whiskers were too short to be called a beard and his nose was so varicose it looked like a road map. We were too far from him to smell, but I was sure he smelled. His hands waved and flapped on loose wrists. "Hi there, baby. Hi there, big boy. I see ya, buster," the man said to Erik. My husband and I exchanged looks, "What do we do?" Erik continued to laugh and answer, "Hi."

Everyone in the restaurant noticed and looked at us and then at the man. The old geezer was creating a nuisance with my beautiful baby. Our meal came and the man began shouting from across the room, "Do ya patty cake? Do you know peek-a-boo? Hey, look, he knows peek-a-boo."

Nobody thought the old man was cute. He was obviously drunk. My husband and I were embarrassed. We ate in silence; all except for Erik, who was running through his repertoire for the admiring skid row bum, who in turn, reciprocated with his cute comments. We finally got through the meal and headed for the door. My husband went to pay the check and told me to meet him in the parking lot. The old man sat poised between me and the door. "Lord, just let me out of here before he speaks to me or Erik," I prayed.

As I drew closer to the man, I turned my back trying to sidestep him and avoid any air he might be breathing. As I did, Erik leaned over my arm, reaching with both arms in a baby's "pick-me-up" position. Before I could stop him, Erik had propelled himself from my arms to the man's. Suddenly a very old smelly man and a very young baby consummated their love and kinship. Erik in an act of total trust, love, and submission laid his tiny head upon the man's ragged shoulder. The man's eyes closed, and I saw tears hover beneath his lashes. His aged hands full of grime, pain, and hard labor, cradled my baby's bottom and stroked his back. No two beings have ever loved so deeply for so short a time. I stood awestruck. The old man rocked and cradled Erik in his arms and his eyes opened and set squarely on mine.

He said in a firm commanding voice, "You take care of this baby." Somehow I managed, "I will," from a throat that contained a stone. He pried Erik from his chest, lovingly and longingly, as though he were in pain. I received my baby, and the man said, "God bless you, ma'am, you've given me my Christmas gift." I said nothing more than a muttered thanks. With Erik in my arms, I ran for the car. My husband was wondering why I was crying and holding Erik so tightly, and why I was saying, "My God, my God, forgive me."

I had just witnessed Christ's love shown through the innocence of a tiny child who saw no sin, who made no judgment; a child who saw a soul, and a mother who saw a suit of clothes. I was a Christian who was blind, holding a child who was not. I felt it was God asking, "Are you willing to share your son for a moment?" when He shared His for all eternity. The ragged old man, unwittingly, had reminded me, "To enter the Kingdom of God, we must become as little children."

I am "moved" by that story—I would guess, much as hearers of The Word were in Jesus' day. In this new millennium, maybe more than ever, people need to hear the truth and find direction for living caring, compassionate, productive, satisfied, humble, happy, fulfilled, victorious, and hopeful lives... with Jesus as Lord!

So what can you look for in this Bible story? First, here is a simple account of the beginning of the Christian faith—it all started with Jesus. The passages are familiar and yet "new"...pulled out of context and in various versions. A lot of the Bible is left out because of duplication, extensive elaboration, historical detail and profound complexity... among other reasons. Yet here is a reference for your most loved passages and one way to integrate the "scattered jewels" of scripture into an artistic and majestic whole. Here's a story—as mind-boggling as eternity and as earthy as a new-born baby...as basic as a piece of bread and as scrumptious as a feast—fit for a King! Here is "easy reading" at its finest and a book hard to put down as each passage propels itself into the next. Still, the reader will not lose momentum by stopping or pausing at any point. On the other hand, selections have no perfect place in this story. Be mindful of the fact that almost every portion of scripture could be placed under any number of chapter titles… since each one has multiple subjects and references. Draw your own conclusions as to where a passage could or should be located.

Above all, enjoy your reading and contemplation. Let yourself be "moved"! Use this story book, inspirational testimony, reference work and life-style handbook to enhance your journey into the Kingdom of God.

A BIBLE STORY

Christian Highlights
The Bible For The 20th Century
Good News For Life And Living
Your Favorite Passages
Inspirational Insights!
The Best Of The Best
The Way To Love
The Gift Of Love

CHAPTERS

A Bible Story

JESUS ARRIVES...

In the beginning was the Word, and the Word was with God, and the Word was God. He was in the beginning with God; all things were made through him, and without him was not anything made that was made. In him was life, and the life was the light of men. The light shines in the darkness, and the darkness has not overcome it.
John 1: 1-5 RSV~

This is how the birth of Jesus Christ took place. His mother Mary was engaged to Joseph, but before they were married, she found out that she was going to have a baby by the Holy Spirit. Joseph was a man who always did what was right, but he did not want to disgrace Mary publicly; so he made plans to break the engagement privately. While he was thinking about this, an angel of the Lord appeared to him in a dream and said, "Joseph, descendant of David, do not be afraid to take Mary to be your wife. For it is by the Holy Spirit that she has conceived. She will have a son, and you will name him Jesus—because he will save his people from their sins." Now all this happened in order to make come true what the Lord had said through the prophet, "A virgin will become pregnant and have a son, and he will be called Immanuel" (which means, "God is with us"). So when Joseph woke up, he married Mary, as the angel of the Lord had told him to. **Matthew 1: 18-24 GNB**

And Joseph also went up from Galilee, from the city of Nazareth, to Judea, to the city of David, which is called Bethlehem, because he was of the house and lineage of David, to be enrolled with Mary, his betrothed, who was with child. And while they were there, the time came for her to be delivered. And she gave birth to her first-born son and wrapped him in swaddling cloths, and laid him in a manger, because there was no place for them in the inn.

And in that region there were shepherds out in the field, keeping watch over their flock by night. And an angel of the Lord appeared to them, and the glory of the Lord shone around them, and they were filled with fear. And the angel said to them, "Be not afraid; for behold, I bring you good news of a great joy which will come to all the people; for to you is born this day in the city of David a Savior, who is Christ the Lord. And this will be a sign for you: you will find a babe wrapped in swaddling cloths and lying in a manger." And suddenly there was with the angel a multitude of the heavenly host praising God and saying, "Glory to God in the highest, and on earth peace among men with whom he is pleased!"

Luke 2: 4-14 RSV
When the angels had left them and gone into heaven, the shepherds said to one another, "Let's go to Bethlehem and see this thing that has happened, which the Lord has told us about." So they hurried off and found Mary and Joseph, and the baby, who was lying in the manger. When they had seen him, they spread the word concerning what had been told them about this child, and all who heard it were amazed at what the shepherds said to them. But Mary treasured up all these things and pondered them in her heart. The shepherds returned, glorifying and praising God for all the things they had heard and seen, which were just as they had been told. **Luke 2: 15-20 NIV**

There appeared a man named John, sent from God; he came as a witness to testify to the light, that all might become believers through him. He was not himself the light; he came to bear witness to the light. The real light which enlightens every man was even then coming into the world. He was in the world; but the world, though it owed its being to him, did not recognize him. He entered his own realm, and his own would not receive him. But to all who did receive him, to those who have yielded him their allegiance, he gave the right to become children of God, not born of any human stock, or by the fleshly desire of a human father, but the offspring of God himself. So the Word became flesh; he came to dwell among us, and we saw his glory, such glory as befits the Father's only Son, full of grace and truth.

Here is John's testimony to him: he cried aloud, 'This is the man I meant when I said, "He comes after me, but takes rank before me"; for before I was born, he already was.' Out of his full store we have all received grace upon grace; for while the Law was given through Moses, grace and truth came through Jesus Christ. No one has ever seen God; but God's only Son, he who is nearest to the Father's heart, he has made him known.
John 1: 6-18 NEB

JESUS IS GOD'S SON

And the Word became flesh and dwelt among us, full of grace and truth; we have beheld his glory, glory as of the only Son from the Father. **John 1: 14 RSV**

There was at that time in Jerusalem a man called Simeon. This man was upright and devout, one who watched and waited for the restoration of Israel, and the Holy Spirit was upon him. It had been disclosed to him by the Holy Spirit that he would not see death until he had seen the Lord's Messiah. Guided by the Spirit he came into the temple; and when the parents brought in the child Jesus to do for him what was customary under the Law, he took him in his arms, praised God, and said: 'This day, Master, thou givest thy servant his discharge in peace; now thy promise is fulfilled. For I have seen with my own eyes the deliverance which thou hast made ready in full view of all the nations: a light that will be a revelation to the heathen, and glory to thy people Israel.' The child's father and mother were full of wonder at what was being said about him. Simeon blessed them and said to Mary his mother, 'This child is destined to be a sign which men reject; and you too shall be pierced to the heart. Many in Israel will stand or fall because of him, and thus the secret thoughts of many will be laid bare.'

Luke 2: 25-35 NEB

When they had done everything prescribed in the law of the Lord, they returned to Galilee to their own town of Nazareth. The child grew big and strong and full of wisdom; and God's favor was upon him. Now it was the practice of his parents to go to Jerusalem every year for the Passover festival; and when he was twelve, they made the pilgrimage as usual. When the festive season was over and they started for home, the boy Jesus stayed behind in Jerusalem. His parents did not know of this; but thinking that he was with the party they journeyed on for a whole day, and only then did they begin looking for him among their friends and relations. As they could not find him they returned to Jerusalem to look for him; and after three days they found him sitting in the temple surrounded by the teachers, listening to them and putting questions; and all who heard him were amazed at his intelligence and the answers he gave. His parents were astonished to see him there, and his mother said to him, 'My son, why have you treated us like this? Your father and I have been searching for you in great anxiety.' 'What made you search?' he said. 'Did you not know that I was bound to be in my Father's house?' But they did not understand what he meant. Then he went back with them to Nazareth, and continued to be under their authority; his mother treasured up all these things in her heart. As Jesus grew up he advanced in wisdom and in favor with God and men. **Luke 2: 39-52 NEB**

In those days came John the Baptist, preaching in the wilderness of Judea, "Repent, for the kingdom of heaven is at hand." For this is he who was spoken of by the prophet Isaiah when he said, "The voice of one crying in the wilderness: Prepare the way of the Lord, make his paths straight." **Matthew 3: 1-3 RSV**

And he went all over the Jordan valley proclaiming a baptism in token of repentance for the forgiveness of sins, as it is written in the book of the prophecies of Isaiah: 'A voice crying aloud in the wilderness, "Prepare a way for the Lord; clear a straight path for him. Every ravine shall be filled in, and every mountain and hill leveled; the corners shall be straightened, and the rugged ways made smooth; and all mankind shall see God's deliverance."' **Luke 3: 3-6 NEB**

And there went out to him all the country of Judea, and all the people of Jerusalem; and they were baptized by him in the river Jordan, confessing their sins. Now John was clothed with camel's hair, and had a leather girdle around his waist, and ate locusts and wild honey. And he preached, saying, "After me comes he who is mightier than I, the thong of whose sandals I am not

worthy to stoop down and untie. I have baptized you with water; but he will baptize you with the Holy Spirit."
Mark 1: 5-8 RSV

The next day John saw Jesus coming toward him and said, "Look, the Lamb of God, who takes away the sin of the world! This is the one I meant when I said, 'A man who comes after me has surpassed me because he was before me.' I myself did not know him, but the reason I came baptizing with water was that he might be revealed to Israel." Then John gave this testimony: "I saw the Spirit come down from heaven as a dove and remain on him. I would not have known him, except that the one who sent me to baptize with water told me, 'The man on whom you see the Spirit come down and remain is he who will baptize with the Holy Spirit.' I have seen and I testify that this is the Son of God."
John 1: 29-34 NIV

In those days Jesus came from Nazareth of Galilee and was baptized by John in the Jordan. And when he came up out of the water, immediately he saw the heavens opened and the Spirit descending upon him like a dove, and a voice came from heaven, "Thou art my beloved Son; with thee I am well pleased."
Mark 1: 9-11 RSV

Full of the Holy Spirit, Jesus returned from the Jordan, and for forty days was led by the Spirit up and down the wilderness and tempted by the devil. All that time

he had nothing to eat, and at the end of it he was famished. The devil said to him, 'If you are the Son of God, tell this stone to become bread.' Jesus answered, 'Scripture says, "Man cannot live on bread alone."' Next the devil led him up and showed him in a flash all the kingdoms of the world. 'All this dominion will I give to you,' he said, 'and the glory that goes with it; for it has been put in my hands and I can give it to anyone I choose. You have only to do homage to me and it shall be yours.' Jesus answered him, 'Scripture says, "You shall do homage to the Lord your God and worship him alone."' The devil took him to Jerusalem and set him on the parapet of the temple. 'If you are the Son of God,' he said, 'throw yourself down; for Scripture says, "He will give his angels orders to take care of you", and again "They will support you in their arms for fear you should strike your foot against a stone."' Jesus answered him, 'It has been said, "You are not to put the Lord your God to the test."' So having come to the end of all his temptations, the devil departed, biding his time.
Luke 4: 1-12 NEB

And he came to Nazareth, where he had been brought up; and he went to the synagogue as his custom was, on the Sabbath day. And he stood up to read; and there was given to him the book of the prophet Isaiah. He opened the book and found the place where it was written, "The Spirit of the Lord is upon me, because he has anointed me to preach good news to the poor. He has sent me to proclaim release to the captives and recovering of sight to the blind, to set at liberty those who are oppressed, to proclaim the acceptable year of the Lord." And he closed the book, and gave it back to the attendant, and sat down; and the eyes of all in the synagogue were fixed on him. And he began to say to them, "Today this scripture has been fulfilled in your hearing." **Luke 4: 16-21 RSV**

At daybreak Jesus left the town and went off to a lonely place. The people started looking for him, and when they found him, they tried to keep him from leaving. But he said to them, "I must preach the Good News of the Kingdom of God in other towns also, because that is what God sent me to do." So he preached in the synagogues throughout the country. **Luke 4: 42-44 GNB**

One day Jesus was standing on the shore of Lake Gennesaret while the people pushed their way up to him to listen to the word of God. He saw two boats pulled up on the beach; the fishermen had left them and were washing the nets. Jesus got into one of the boats—it belonged to Simon—and asked him to push off a little from the shore. Jesus sat in the boat and taught the crowd. When he finished speaking, he said to Simon, "Push the boat out further to the deep water, and you and your partners let down your nets for a catch." "Master," Simon answered, "we worked hard all night long and caught nothing. But if you say so, I will let down the nets." They let them down and caught such a large number of fish that the nets were about to break. So they motioned to their partners in the other boat to come and help them. They came and filled both boats so full of fish that the boats were about to sink. When Simon Peter saw what had happened, he fell on his knees before Jesus and said, "Go away from me, Lord! I am a sinful man!"

He and the others with him were all amazed at the large number of fish they had caught. The same was true of Simon's partners, James and John, the sons of Zebedee. Jesus said to Simon, "Don't be afraid; from now on you will be catching men." They pulled the boats up on the beach, left everything, and followed Jesus.
Luke 5: 1-11 GNB

After this, Jesus went out and saw a tax collector by the name of Levi sitting at his tax booth. "Follow me," Jesus said to him, and Levi got up, left everything and followed him. Then Levi held a great banquet for Jesus at his house, and a large crowd of tax collectors and others were eating with them. But the Pharisees and the teachers of the law who belonged to their sect complained to his disciples, "Why do you eat and drink with tax collectors and 'sinners'?" Jesus answered them, "It is not the healthy who need a doctor, but the sick. I have not come to call the righteous, but sinners to repentance."
Luke 5: 27-32 NIV+

Two days later there was a wedding in the town of Cana

in Galilee. Jesus' mother was there, and Jesus and his disciples had also been invited to the wedding. When the wine had given out, Jesus' mother said to him, "They are out of wine." "You must not tell me what to do," Jesus replied. "My time has not yet come." Jesus' mother then told the servants, "Do whatever he tells you."

The Jews have rules about ritual washing, and for this purpose six stone water jars were there, each one large enough to hold between twenty and thirty gallons. Jesus said to the servants, "Fill these jars with water." They filled them to the brim, and then he told them, "Now draw some water out and take it to the man in charge of the feast." They took him the water, which now had turned into wine, and he tasted it. He did not know where this wine had come from (but, of course, the servants who had drawn out the water knew); so he called the bridegroom and said to him, "Everyone else serves the best wine first, and after the guests have drunk a lot, he serves the ordinary wine. But you have kept the best wine until now!" Jesus performed this first miracle in Cana in Galilee; there he revealed his glory, and his disciples believe in him. **John 2: 1-11 GNB**

Then he said to them all, "If anyone wants to become my follower, he must deny himself, take up his cross daily, and follow me. For whoever wants to save his life will lose it, but whoever loses his life for my sake will save it. For what does it benefit a person if he gains the whole world but loses or forfeits himself? **Luke 9: 23-25 NET**

Approximately eight days after these sayings, Jesus took Peter, John and James with him and went up the hill to pray. While he was praying, he was changed in appearance and his clothes became very bright and white. Two men—Moses and Elijah—were talking with Jesus. They had a heavenly appearance and they spoke about how Jesus must go to Jerusalem and carry out his mission. But Peter and his friends were sleepy and as they tried to wake up they saw the special vision of Jesus and the two men who were with him. Just as they were about to leave, Peter said to Jesus, "Lord, it's wonderful to be here. Let's make three shelters—one for each of you" —not realizing what he was saying. As he was speaking, a cloud drifted over them, and they were afraid. Then a voice came out of the cloud and said, "This is my Son, my special Chosen One! Listen to what he tells you!" When the voice was gone, Jesus was alone. This was so overwhelming that Peter and his two friends were silent about all they had witnessed. **Luke 9: 28-36 HOV**

It was almost time for the Passover Festival, so Jesus went to Jerusalem. There in the Temple he found men selling cattle, sheep, and pigeons, and also the moneychangers sitting at their table. So he made a whip from cords and drove all the animals out of the Temple, both the sheep and the cattle; he overturned the tables of the moneychangers and scattered their coins; and he ordered the men who sold the pigeons, "Take them out of here! Stop making my Father's house a marketplace!" His disciples remembered that the scripture says, "My devotion to your house, O God, burns in me like a fire." **John 2: 13-17 GNB**

And he went about all Galilee, teaching in their synagogues and preaching the gospel of the kingdom and healing every disease and every infirmity among the people. So his fame spread throughout all Syria, and they brought him all the sick, those afflicted with various diseases and pains, demoniacs, epileptics, and paralytics, and he healed them. And great crowds followed him from Galilee and the Decapolis and Jerusalem and Judea and from beyond the Jordan. **Matthew 4: 23-25 RSV**

Then Jesus went back to Cana in Galilee, where he had turned the water into wine. A government official was there whose son was sick in Capernaum. When he heard that Jesus had come from Judea to Galilee, he went to him and asked him to go to Capernaum and heal his son, who was about to die. Jesus said to him, "None of you will ever believe unless you see miracles and wonders." "Sir," replied the official, "come with me before my child dies." Jesus said to him, "Go; your son will live!" The man believed Jesus' words and went. On his way home his servants met him with the news, "Your boy is going to live!" He asked them what time it was when his son got better, and they answered, "It was one o'clock yesterday afternoon when the fever left him." Then the father remembered that it was at that very hour when Jesus told him, "Your son will live." So he and all his family believed. **John 4: 46-53 GNB**

Jesus went across Lake Galilee (or, Lake Tiberias, as it is also called). A large crowd followed him, because they had seen his miracles of healing the sick. Jesus went up a hill and sat down with his disciples. The time for the Passover Festival was near. Jesus looked around and saw that a large crowd was coming to him, so he asked Philip, "Where can we buy enough food to feed all these people?" (He said this to test Philip; actually he already knew what he would do.) Philip answered, "For everyone to have even a little, it would take more than two hundred silver coins to buy enough bread."

Another one of his disciples, Andrew, who was Simon Peter's brother, said, "There is a boy here who had five loaves of barley bread and two fish. But they will certainly not be enough for all these people." "Make the people sit down," Jesus told them. (There was a lot of grass there.) So all the people sat down; there were about five thousand men. Jesus took the bread, gave thanks to God, and distributed it to the people who were sitting there. He did the same with the fish, and they all had as much as they wanted. When they were all full, he said to his disciples, "Gather the pieces left over; let us not waste a bit." So they gathered them all and filled twelve baskets with the pieces left over from the five barley loaves which the people had eaten. **John 6: 1-13 GNB**

When they found him on the other side of the lake, they asked him, "Rabbi, when did you get here?" Jesus answered, "I tell you the truth, you are looking for me, not because you saw miraculous signs but because you ate the loaves and had your fill. Do not work for food that spoils, but for food that endures to eternal life, which the Son of Man will give you. On him God the Father has placed his seal of approval." Then they asked him, "What must we do to do the works God requires?" Jesus answered, "The work of God is this: to believe in the one he has sent." **John 6: 25-29 NIV**

They said, 'What sign can you give us to see, so that we may believe you? What is the work you do? Out ancestors had manna to eat in the desert; as Scripture says, "He gave them bread from heaven to eat."' Jesus answered, 'I tell you this: the truth is, not that Moses gave you the bread from heaven, but that my Father gives you the real bread from heaven. The bread that God gives comes down from heaven and brings life to the world.' They said to him, 'Sir, give us this bread now and always.' Jesus said to them, 'I am the bread of life. Whoever comes to me shall never be hungry, and whoever believes in me shall never be thirsty. But you, as I said, do not believe although you have seen. All that the Father gives me will come to me, and the man who comes to me I will never turn away. I have

come down from heaven, not to do my own will, but the will of him who sent me. It is his will that I should not lose even one of all that he has given me, but raise them all up on the last day. For it is my Father's will that everyone who looks upon the Son and puts his faith in him shall possess eternal life; and I will raise him up on the last day.'
John 6: 30-40 NEB+

Then Jesus cried out, "When a man believes in me, he does not believe in me only, but in the one who sent me. When he looks at me, he sees the one who sent me. I have come into the world as a light, so that no one who believes in me should stay in darkness. "As for the person who hears my words but does not keep them, I do not judge him. For I did not come to judge the world, but to save it. There is a judge for the one who rejects me and does not accept my words; that very word which I spoke will condemn him at the last day. For I did not speak of my own accord, but the Father who sent me commanded me what to say and how to say it. I know that his command leads to eternal life. So whatever I say is just what the Father has told me to say."
John 12: 44-50 NIV

Christ is the visible likeness of he invisible God. He is the first-born Son, superior to all created things. For through him God created everything in heaven and on earth, the seen and the unseen things, including spiritual powers, lords, rulers, and authorities. God created the whole universe through him and for him. Christ existed before all things, and in union with him all things have their proper place. He is the head of his body, the church; he is the source of the body's life. He is the first-born Son, who was raised from death, in order that he alone might have the first place in all things. For it was by God's own decision that the Son has in himself the full nature of God. Through the Son, then, God decided to bring the whole universe back to himself. God made peace through his Son's death on the cross and so brought back to himself all things, both on earth and in heaven.

At one time you were far away from God and were his enemies because of the evil things you did and thought. But now, by means of the physical death of his Son, God has made you his friends, in order to bring you, holy, pure, and faultless, into his presence. You must, of course, continue faithful on a firm and sure foundation, and must not allow yourselves to be shaken from the hope you gained when you heard the gospel. It is of this gospel that I, Paul, became a servant—this gospel which has been preached to everybody in the world.
Colossians 1: 15-23 GNB~

For in Christ all the fullness of the Deity lives in bodily form, and you have been given fullness in Christ, who is the head over every power and authority.
Colossians 2: 9-10 NIV

In many and various ways God spoke of old to our fathers by the prophets; but in these last days he has spoken to us by a Son, whom he appointed the heir of all things, through whom also he created the world. He reflects the glory of God and bears the very stamp of his nature, upholding the universe by his word of power. When he had made purification for sins, he sat down at the right hand of the Majesty on high, having become as much superior to angels as the name he has obtained is more excellent than theirs. **Hebrews 1 :1-4 RSV**

JESUS SPEAKS WITH AUTHORITY!

Seeing the crowds, he went up on the mountain, and when he sat down his disciples came to him. And he opened his mouth and taught them, saying: "Blessed are the poor in spirit, for theirs is the kingdom of heaven. Blessed are those who morn, for they shall be comforted. Blessed are the meek, for they shall inherit the earth. Blessed are those who hunger and thirst for righteousness, for they shall be satisfied. Blessed are the merciful, for they shall obtain mercy. Blessed are the pure in heart, for they shall see God. Blessed are the peacemakers, for they shall be called sons of God. Blessed are those who are persecuted for righteousness' sake, for theirs is the kingdom of heaven. Blessed are you when men revile you and persecute you and utter all kinds of evil against you falsely on my account. Rejoice and be glad, for your reward is great in heaven, for so men persecuted the prophets who were before you." **Matthew 5: 1-12 RSV***

"You are the salt of the earth; but if salt has lost its

taste, how shall its saltness be restored? It is no longer good for anything except to be thrown out and trodden under foot by men. You are the light of the world. A city set on a hill cannot be hid. Nor do men light a lamp and put it under a bushel, but on a stand, and it gives light to all in the house. Let your light so shine before men, that they may see your good works and give glory to your Father who is in heaven." **Matthew 5: 13-16 RSV~**

"Therefore, if you are offering your gift at the altar and there remember that your brother has something against you, leave your gift there in front of the altar. First go and be reconciled to your brother; then come and offer your gift. **Matthew 5: 23-24 NIV**

"You have heard that it was said, 'An eye for an eye and a tooth for a tooth.' But I say to you, Do not resist one who is evil. But if any one strikes you on the right cheek, turn to him the other also; and if any one would sue you and take your coat, let him have your cloak as well; and if any one forces you to go one mile, go with him two miles." **Matthew 5: 38-41 RSV**

"You have heard that it was said, 'You shall love your neighbor and hate your enemy.' But I say to you, Love your enemies and pray for those who persecute you, so that you may be sons of your Father who is in heaven; for he makes his sun rise on the evil and on the good, and sends rain on the just and on the unjust. For if you love those who love you, what reward have you? Do not even the tax collectors do the same? **Matthew 5: 43-46 RSV+**

"Beware of practicing your piety before men in order to be seen by them; for then you will have no reward from your Father who is in heaven." **Matthew 6: 1 RSV**

"And when you pray, you must not be like the hypocrites; for they love to stand and pray in the synagogues and at the street corners, that they may be seen by men. Truly, I say to you, they have their reward. But when you pray, go into your room and shut the door and pray to your Father who is in secret; and your Father who sees in secret will reward you.

"And in praying do not heap up empty phrases as the Gentiles do; for they think that they will be heard for their many words. Do not be like them, for your Father knows what you need before you ask him. Pray then like this: Our Father who art in heaven, Hallowed be thy name. Thy kingdom come, Thy will be done, On earth as it is in heaven. Give us this day our daily bread; And forgive us our debts, As we also have forgiven our debtors; And lead us not into temptation, But deliver us from evil." **Matthew 6: 7-13 RSV***

"Do not store up for yourselves treasures on earth, where moth and rust destroy, and where thieves break in and steal. But store up for yourselves treasures in heaven, where moth and rust do not destroy, and where thieves do not break in and steal. For where your treasure is, there your heart will be also." **Matthew 6: 19-21 NIV**

"No one can serve two masters; for either he will hate the one and love the other, or he will be devoted to the one and despise the other. You cannot serve God and mammon."

"Therefore I tell you, do not be anxious about your life, what you shall eat or what you shall drink, nor about your body, what you shall put on. Is not life more than food, and the body more than clothing? Look at the birds of the air: they neither sow nor reap nor gather into barns, and yet your heavenly Father feeds them. Are you not of more value than they? And which of you by being anxious can add one cubit to his span of life? And why are you anxious about clothing? Consider the lilies of the field, how they grow; they neither toil nor spin; yet I tell you, even Solomon in all his glory was not arrayed like one of these. But if God so clothes the grass of the field, which today is alive and tomorrow is thrown into the oven, will he not much more clothe you, O men of little faith? Therefore do not be anxious, saying, 'What shall we eat?' or 'What shall we drink?' or 'What shall we wear?' For the Gentiles seek all these things; and your heavenly Father knows that you need them all. But seek first his kingdom and his righteousness, and all these things shall be yours as well." **Matthew 6: 25-33 RSV**

"Judge not, that you be not judged. For with the judgment you pronounce you will be judged, and the measure you give will be the measure you get. Why do you see the speck that is in your brother's eye, but do not notice the log that is in your own eye? Or how can you say to your brother, 'Let me take the speck out of your eye,' when there is the log in your own eye? You hypocrite, first take the log out of your own eye, and then you will see clearly to take the speck out of your brother's eye." **Matthew 7: 1-5 RSV**

"Ask and it will be given to you; seek and you will find; knock and the door will be opened to you. For everyone who asks receives; he who seeks finds; and to him who knocks, the door will be opened." **Matthew 7: 7-8 NIV**

"Enter by the narrow gate; for the gate is wide and the way is easy, that leads to destruction, and those who enter by it are many. For the gate is narrow and the way is hard, that leads to life, and those who find it are few." **Matthew 7: 13-14 RSV**

The Pharisees asked him, 'When will the kingdom of God come?' He said, 'You cannot tell by observation when the kingdom of God comes. There will be no saying, "Look, here it is!" or "there it is!"; for in fact the kingdom of God is among you.' **Luke 17: 20-21 NEB**

"Every one then who hears these words of mine and does them will be like a wise man who built his house upon the rock; and the rain fell, and the floods came, and the winds blew and beat upon that house, but it did not fall, because it had been founded on the rock. And every one who hears these words of mine and does not do them will be like a foolish man who built his house upon the sand; and the rain fell, and the floods came, and the winds blew and beat against that house, and it fell; and great was the fall of it." **Matthew 7: 24-27 RSV**

"Do not be worried and upset," Jesus told them. "Believe in God and believe also in me. There are many rooms in my Father's house, and I am going to prepare a place for you. I would not tell you this if it were not so. And after I go and prepare a place for you, I will come back and take you to myself, so that you will be where I am. You know the way that leads to the place where I am going." Thomas said to him, "Lord, we do not know where you are going; so how can we know the way to get there?" Jesus answered him, "I am the way, the truth and the life; no one goes to the Father except by me. Now that you have known me," he said to them, "you will know my Father also, and from now on you do know him and you have seen him." **John 14: 1-7 GNB**

That same day Jesus went out of the house and sat beside the sea. And great crowds gathered about him, so that he got into a boat and sat there; and the whole crowd stood on the beach. And he told them many things in parables, saying: "A sower went out to sow. And as he sowed, some seeds fell along the path, and the birds came and devoured them. Other seeds fell on rocky ground, where they had not much soil, and immediately they sprang up, since they had no depth of soil, but when the sun rose they were scorched; and since they had no root they withered away. Other seeds fell upon the thorns, and the thorns grew up and choked them. Other seeds fell on good soil and brought forth grain, some a hundredfold, some sixty, some thirty. He who has ears, let him hear. **"Matthew 13: 1-9 RSV**

"Hear then the parable of the sower. When any one hears the word of the kingdom and does not understand it, the evil one comes and snatches away what is sown in his heart; this is what was sown along the path. As for what was sown on rocky ground, this is he who hears the word and immediately received it with joy; yet he has no root in himself, but endures for a while, and when tribulation or persecution arises on account of the word, immediately he falls away. As for what was sown among thorns, this is he who hears the word, but the cares of the world and the delight in riches choke the word, and it proves unfruitful. As for what was sown on good soil, this is he who hears the word and understands it; he indeed bears fruit, and yields, in one case a hundredfold, in another sixty, and in another thirty." **Matthew 13: 18-23 RSV**

Philip said to him, "Lord, reveal the Father to us and we will be satisfied." Jesus responded, "I've been with you so long, and yet you don't know me, Philip? The person who has seen me has already seen the Father. How can you say to me, 'Reveal the Father to us'? Don't you believe that we are together and live in one another?

What I am speaking are not only my own words, but they also come from the Father, who carries out all his wonderful work through me. Do you believe me when I tell you that I am in the Father and the Father is in me? If you don't believe, be convinced because of the works themselves. The truth is that the person who believes in me will be able to carry out the same things as I perform, and even greater ones, because I am going to be with the Father. Be certain that you will be able to do anything you ask in my name, so that the Father will be glorified in his Son. Ask anything in my name, and I will see that it's done. **John 14: 8-14 HOV**

JESUS' DEATH AND RESURRECTION

Jesus was at Bethany, in the house of Simon the leper. As he sat at table, a woman came in carrying a small bottle of very costly perfume, pure oil of nard. She broke it open and poured the oil over his head. Some of those present said to one another angrily, 'Why this waste? The perfume might have been sold for thirty pounds and the money given to the poor'; and they turned upon her with fury. But Jesus said, 'Let her alone. Why must you make trouble for her? It is a fine thing she has done for me. You have the poor among you always, and you can help them whenever you like; but you will not always have me. She has done what lay in her power; she is beforehand with anointing my body for burial. I tell you this: wherever in all the world the Gospel is proclaimed, what she has done will be told as her memorial.'
Mark 14: 3-9 NEB

Then, six days before the Passover, Jesus came to Bethany, where Lazarus lived, whom he had raised from the dead. So they prepared a dinner for Jesus there. Martha was serving, and Lazarus was among those present at the table with him. Then Mary took three quarters of a pound of expensive aromatic oil from pure nard and anointed the feet of Jesus. She then wiped his feet dry with her hair. (Now the house was filled with the fragrance of the perfumed oil.) But Judas Iscariot, one of his disciples (the one who was going to betray him) said, "Why wasn't this oil sold for three hundred silver coins and the money given to the poor?" (Now Judas said this not because he was concerned about the poor, but because he was a thief. As keeper of the money box, he used to steal what was put into it.) So Jesus said, "Leave her alone. She has kept it for the day of my burial. For you will always have the poor with you, but you will not always have me!" **John 12: 1-8 NET**

"In a little while you will not see me any more, and then a little while later you will see me." Some of his disciples asked among themselves, "What does this mean? He tells us that in a little while we will not see him, and then a little while later we will see him; and he also says, 'It is because I am going to the Father.' What does this 'a little while' mean? We don't know what he is talking about!"

Jesus knew that they wanted to question him, so he said to them, "I said, 'In a little while you will not see me, and then a little while later you will see me.' Is this what you are asking about among yourselves? I am telling you the truth: you will cry and weep, but the world will be glad; you will be sad, but your sadness will turn into gladness. When a woman is about to give birth, she is sad because her hour of suffering has come; but when the baby is born, she forgets her suffering, because she is happy that a baby has been born into the world. That is how it is with you: now you are sad, but I will see you again, and your hearts will be filled with gladness, the kind of gladness that no one can take away from you. **John 16: 16-22 GNB**

And when they drew near to Jerusalem and came to Bethphage, to the Mount of Olives, then Jesus sent two disciples, saying to them, "Go into the village opposite you, and immediately you will fine an ass tied, and a colt with her; untie them and bring them to me. If any one says anything to you, you shall say, 'The Lord has need of them,' and he will send them immediately." This took place to fulfill what was spoken by the prophet, saying, "Tell the daughter of Zion, Behold, your king is coming to you, humble, and mounted on an ass, and on a colt, the foal of an ass."

The disciples went and did as Jesus had directed them; they brought the ass and the colt, and put their garments on them, and he sat thereon. Most of the crowd spread their garments on the road, and others cut branches from the trees and spread them on the road. And the crowds that went before him and that followed him shouted, "Hosanna to the Son of David! Blessed be he who comes in the name of the Lord! Hosanna in the highest!" **Matthew 21: 1-9 RSV**

It was now the day before the Passover Festival. Jesus knew that the hour had come for him to leave this world and go to the Father. He had always loved those in the world who were his own, and he loved them to the very end.

Jesus and his disciples were at supper. The Devil had already put the thought of betraying Jesus into the heart of Judas, the son of Simon Iscariot. Jesus knew that the Father had given him complete power; he knew that he had come from God and was going to God. So he rose from the table, took off his outer garment, and tied a towel around his waist. Then he poured some water into a washbasin and began to wash the disciples' feet and dry them with the towel around his waist. He came to Simon Peter, who said to him, "Are you going to wash my feet, Lord?" Jesus answered him, "You do not understand now what I am doing, but you will understand later." Peter declared, "Never at any time will you wash my feet!" "If I do not wash your feet," Jesus answered, "you will no longer be my disciple." Simon Peter answered, "Lord, do not wash only my feet, then! Wash my hands and head, too!" Jesus said, "Anyone who has taken a bath is completely clean and does not have to wash himself, except for his feet. All of you are clean—all except one." (Jesus already knew who was going to betray him; that is why he said, "All of you, except one, are clean.")

After Jesus had washed their feet, he put his outer garment back on and returned to his place at the table. "Do you understand what I have just done to you?" he asked. "You call me Teacher and Lord, and it is right that you do so, because that is what I am. I, your Lord and Teacher, have just washed your feet. You, then, should wash one another's feet. I have set an example for you, so that you will do just what I have done for you. I am telling you the truth: no slave is greater than his master, and no messenger is greater than the one who sent him. Now that you know this truth, how happy you will be if you put it into practice!" **John 13: 1-17 GNB**

When he had said these things, Jesus was greatly distressed in spirit, and testified, "I tell you the solemn truth, one of you will betray me." The disciples began to look at one another, worried and perplexed to know which of them he was talking about. One of his disciples, the one Jesus loved, was at the table to the right of Jesus in a place of honor. So Simon Peter gestured to this disciple to ask Jesus who it was he was referring to. Then the disciple whom Jesus loved leaned back against Jesus' chest and asked him, "Lord, who is it?" Jesus replied, "It is the one to whom I will give this piece of bread after I have dipped it in the dish." Then he dipped the piece of bread in the dish and gave it to

Judas Iscariot, Simon's son. And after Judas took the piece of bread, Satan entered into him. Jesus said to him, "What you are about to do, do quickly." (Now none of those present at the table understood why Jesus said this to Judas. Some thought that, because Judas had the money box, Jesus was telling him to buy whatever they needed for the feast, or to give something to the poor.) Judas took the piece of bread and went out immediately. (Now it was night.)

When Judas had gone out, Jesus said, "Now the Son of Man is glorified, and God is glorified in him. If God is glorified in him, God will also glorify him in himself, and he will glorify him right away. Children, I am still with you for a little while. You will look for me, and just as I said to the Jewish religious leaders, 'Where I am going you cannot come,' now I tell you the same. "I give you a new commandment – to love one another. Just as I have loved you, you also are to love one another. Everyone will know by this that you are my disciples – if you have love for one another." Simon Peter said to him, "Lord, where are you going?" Jesus replied, "Where I am going, you cannot follow me now, but you will follow later."

Peter said to him, "Lord, why can't I follow you now? I will lay down my life for you!" Jesus answered, "Will you lay down your life for me? I tell you the solemn truth, the rooster will not crow until you have denied me three times! **John 13: 21-38 NET**

Now the Festival of Unleavened Bread, know as Passover, was approaching, and the chief priests and the doctors of the law were trying to devise some means of doing away with him; for they were afraid of the people. Then Satan entered into Judas Iscariot, who was one of the Twelve; and Judas went to the chief priests and officers of the temple police to discuss ways and means of putting Jesus into their power. They were greatly pleased and undertook to pay him a sum of money. He agreed, and began to look out for an opportunity to betray him to them without collecting a crowd.

Then came the day of Unleavened Bread, on which the Passover victim had to be slaughtered, and Jesus sent Peter and John with these instructions: 'Go and prepare for our Passover supper.' **Luke 22: 1-7 NEB**

While they were eating, Jesus took bread, gave thanks and broke it, and gave it to his disciples, saying, "Take and eat; this is my body." Then he took the cup, gave thanks and offered it to them, saying, "Drink from it, all of you. This is my blood of the covenant, which is poured out for many for the forgiveness of sins. I tell you, I will not drink of this fruit of the vine from now on until that day when I drink it anew with you in my Father's kingdom." **Matthew 26: 26-29 NIV~**

Then he went out and made is way as usual to the Mount of Olives, accompanied by the disciples. When he reached the place he said to them, 'Pray that you may be spared the hour of testing.' He himself withdrew from them about a stone's throw, knelt down, and began to pray: 'Father, if it be thy will, take this cup away from me. Yet not my will but thine be done.' And now there appeared to him an angel from heaven bringing him strength, and in anguish of spirit he prayed the more urgently; and his sweat was like clots of blood falling to the ground. When he rose from prayer and came to the disciples he found them asleep, worn out by grief. 'Why are you sleeping?' he said. 'Rise and pray that you may be spared the test.' While he was still speaking a crowd appeared with the man called Judas, one of the Twelve, at their head. He came up to Jesus to kiss him; but Jesus said, 'Judas, would you betray the Son of Man with a kiss?' **Luke 22: 39-48 NEB**

Jesus knew everything that was going to happen to him, so he stepped forward and asked them, "Who is it you are looking for?" "Jesus of Nazareth," they answered. "I am he," he said. Judas the traitor, was standing there with them. When Jesus said to them, "I am he," they moved back and fell to the ground. Again Jesus asked them, "Who is it you are looking for?" "Jesus of Nazareth," they said. "I have already told you that I am he," Jesus said. "If, then, you are looking for me, let these others go." (He said this so that what he had said might come true: "Father, I have not lost even one of those you gave me.")

Simon Peter, who had a sword, drew it and struck the

High Priest's slave, cutting off his right ear. The name of the slave was Malchus. Jesus said to Peter, "Put your sword back in its place! Do you think that I will not drink the cup of suffering which my Father has given me? **John 18: 4-11 GNB**

Then they arrested him and led him away. They brought him to the High Priest's house, and Peter followed at a distance. They lit a fire in the middle of the courtyard and sat round it, and Peter sat among them. A serving-maid who saw him sitting in the firelight stared at him and said, 'This man was with him too.' But he denied it: 'Woman,' he said, 'I do not know him.' A little later someone else noticed him and said, 'You also are one of them.' But Peter said to him, 'No, I am not.' About an hour passed and another spoke more strongly still: 'Of course this fellow was with him. He must have been; he is a Galilean.' But Peter said, 'Man, I do not know what you are talking about.' At that moment, while he was still speaking, a cock crew; and the Lord turned and looked at Peter. And Peter remembered the Lord's words, 'Tonight before the cock crows you will disown me three times.' **Luke 22: 54-62 NEB**

When day broke, the elders of the nation, chief priests, and doctors of the law assembled, and he was brought before their Council. 'Tell us,' they said, 'are you the Messiah?' 'If I tell you,' he replied, 'you will not believe me; and if I ask questions, you will not answer. But from now on, the Son of Man will be seated at the

right hand of Almighty God.' 'You are the Son of God, then?' they all said, and he replied, 'It is you who say I am.' They said, 'Need we call further witnesses? We have heard it ourselves from his own lips.' With that the whole assembly rose, and they brought him before Pilate. They opened the case against him by saying, 'We found this man subverting our nation, opposing the payment of taxes to Caesar, and claiming to be Messiah, a king.' Pilate asked him, 'Are you the king of the Jews?' He replied, 'The words are yours.' Pilate then said to the chief priests and the crowd, 'I find no case for this man to answer.' But they insisted: 'His teaching is causing disaffection among the people all through Judaea. It started from Galilee and has spread as far as this city.'
Luke 22: 66- 23: 5 NEB

Then Pilate took Jesus and had him whipped. The soldiers made a crown out of thorny branches and put it on his head; then they put a purple robe on him and came to him and said, "Long live the King of the Jews!" And they went up and slapped him. Pilate went back out once more and said to the crowd, "Look, I will bring him out here to you to let you see that I cannot find any reason to condemn him." So Jesus came out, wearing the crown of thorns and the purple robe. Pilate said to them, "Look! Here is the man!"

When the chief priests and the temple guards saw him, they shouted, "Crucify him! Crucify him!" Pilate said to them, "You take him, then, and crucify him. I find no reason to condemn him." The crowd answered back, "We have a law that says he ought to die, because he claimed to be the Son of God." When Pilate heard this, he was even more afraid. He went back into the palace and asked Jesus, "Where do you come from?" But Jesus did not answer. Pilate said to him, "You will not speak to me? Remember, I have authority to set you free and also to have you crucified." Jesus answered, "You have authority over me only because it was given to you by God. So the man who handed me over to you is guilty of a worse sin."

When Pilate heard this, he tried to find a way to set Jesus free. But the crowd shouted back, "If you set him free, that means that you are not the Emperor's friend! Anyone who claims to be a king is a rebel against the Emperor!" When Pilate heard these words, he took Jesus outside and sat down on the judge's seat in the place called, "The Stone Pavement." (In Hebrew the name is "Gabbatha.") It was then almost noon of the day before the Passover. Pilate said to the people, "Here is your king!" They shouted back, "Kill him! Kill him! Crucify him!" Pilate asked them, "Do you want me to crucify your king?" The chief priests answered, "The only king we have is the Emperor!" Then Pilate handed Jesus over to them to be crucified.

So they took charge of Jesus. He went out, carrying his cross, and came to "The Place of the Skull," as it is called. (In Hebrew it is called "Golgotha.") There they crucified him; and they also crucified two other men, one on each side, with Jesus between them. Pilate wrote a notice and had it put on the cross. "Jesus of Nazareth, the King of the Jews," is what he wrote. Many people read it, because the place where Jesus was crucified was not far from the city. The notice was written in Hebrew, Latin, and Greek. The chief priests said to Pilate, "Do not write 'The King of the Jews,' but rather, 'This man said, I am the King of the Jews.'" Pilate answered, "What I have written stays written."

After the soldiers had crucified Jesus, they took his clothes and divided them into four parts, one part for each soldier. They also took the robe, which was made of one piece of woven cloth without any seams in it. The soldiers said to one another, "Let's not tear it; let's throw dice to see who will get it." This happened in order to make the scripture come true: "They divided my clothes among themselves and gambled for my robe." And this is what the soldiers did.

Standing close to Jesus' cross were his mother, his mother's sister, Mary the wife of Clopas, and Mary Magdalene. Jesus saw his mother and the disciple he loved standing there; so he said to his mother, "He is your son." Then he said to the disciple, "She is your mother." From that time the disciple took her to live in his home. **John 19: 1-27 GNB**

One of the criminals who hung there hurled insults at him: "Aren't you the Christ? Save yourself and us!" But the other criminal rebuked him. "Don't you fear God," he said, "since you are under the same sentence? We are punished justly, for we are getting what our deeds deserve. But this man has done nothing wrong." Then he said, "Jesus, remember me when you come into your kingdom." Jesus answered him, "I tell you the truth, today you will be with me in paradise."
Luke 23: 39-43 NIV

The passers-by hurled abuse at him: 'Aha!' they cried wagging their heads, 'you would pull the temple down, would you, and build it in three days? Come down from the cross and save yourself!' So too the chief priests and lawyers jested with one another: 'He saved others,' they said, 'but he cannot save himself. Let the Messiah, the king of Israel, come down now from the cross. If we see that, we shall believe.' Even those who were crucified with him taunted him. **Mark 15: 29-32 NEB**

Jesus knew that by now everything had been completed; and in order to make the scripture come true, he said, "I am thirsty." A bowl was there, full of cheap wine; so a sponge was soaked in the wine, put on a stalk of hyssop, and lifted up to his lips. Jesus drank the wine and said, "It is finished!" Then he bowed his head and died.
John 19: 28-30 GNB

Then, because it was the day of preparation, so that the

bodies should not stay on the crosses on the Sabbath (for that Sabbath was an especially important one), the Jewish leaders asked Pilate to have the victims' legs broken and the bodies taken down. So the soldiers came and broke the legs of the two men who had been crucified with Jesus, first the one and then the other. But when they came to Jesus and saw that he was already dead, they did not break his legs. But one of the soldiers pierced his side with a spear, and blood and water flowed out immediately. And the person who saw it has testified (and his testimony is true, and he knows that he is telling the truth), so that you also may believe. For these things happened so that the scripture would be fulfilled, "Not a bone of his will be broken." And again another scripture says, "They will look on the one whom they have pierced." **John 19: 31-37 NET**

And the curtain of the temple was torn in two from top to bottom. And when the centurion who was standing opposite him saw how he died, he said, 'Truly this man was a son of God.' A number of women were also present, watching from a distance. Among them were Mary of Magdala, Mary the mother of James the younger and of Joseph, and Salome, who had all followed him and waited on him when he was in Galilee, and there were several others who had come up to Jerusalem with him.

By this time evening had come; and as it was Preparation-day (that is, the day before the Sabbath), Joseph of Arimathaea, a respected member of the Council, a man who looked forward to the kingdom of God, bravely went in to Pilate and asked for the body of Jesus. Pilate was surprised to hear that he was already dead; so he sent for the centurion and asked him whether it was long since he died. And when he heard the centurion's report, he gave Joseph leave to take the dead body. **Mark 15: 38-45 NEB**

He was accompanied by Nicodemus, the man who earlier had visited Jesus at night. Nicodemus brought a mixture of myrrh and aloes, about seventy-five pounds. Taking Jesus' body, the two of them wrapped it, with the spices, in strips of linen. This was in accordance with Jewish burial customs. At the place where Jesus was crucified, there was a garden, and in the garden a new tomb, in which no one had ever been laid. Because it was the Jewish day of Preparation and since the tomb was nearby, they laid Jesus there. **John 19: 39-42 NIV**

Early on Sunday morning, while it was still dark, Mary Magdalene went to the tomb and saw that the stone had been taken away from the entrance. She went running to Simon Peter and the other disciple, who Jesus loved, and told them, "They have taken the Lord from the tomb, and we don't know where they have put him."

Then Peter and other disciple went to the tomb. The two of them were running, but the other disciple ran faster than Peter and reached the tomb first. He bent over and saw the linen cloths, but he did not go in.

Behind him came Simon Peter, and he went straight into the tomb. He saw the linen cloths lying there and the cloth which had been around Jesus' head. It was not lying with the linen cloths but was rolled up by itself. Then the other disciple, who had reached the tomb first, also went in; he saw and believed. (They still did not understand the scripture which said that he must rise from death.) Then the disciples went back home. **John 20:1-10 GNB**

But Mary stood outside the tomb weeping. As she wept, she bent down and looked into the tomb. And she saw two angels in white sitting where Jesus' body had been lying, one at the head and one at the feet. They said to her, "Woman, why are you weeping?" Mary replied, "They have taken my Lord away, and I do not know where they have put him!" When she had said this, she turned around and saw Jesus standing there, but she did not know that it was Jesus. Jesus said to her, "Woman, why are you weeping? Who are you looking for?" Because she thought he was the gardener, she said to him, "Sir, if you have carried him away, tell me where you have put him, and I will take him." Jesus said to her, "Mary." She turned and said to him in Aramaic, "*Rabboni*" (which means Teacher). Jesus replied, "Do not touch me, for I have not yet ascended to my Father. Go to my brothers and tell them, 'I am ascending to my Father and your Father, to my God and your God.'" Mary Magdalene came and informed the disciples, "I have seen the Lord!" And she told them what Jesus had said to her. **John 20: 11-18 NET**

That same day two of them were on their way to a village called Emmaus, which lay about seven miles from Jerusalem, and they were talking together about all these happenings. As they talked and discussed it with one another, Jesus himself came up and walked along with them; but something kept them from seeing who it was. He asked them, 'What is it you are debating as you walk?' They halted, their faces full of gloom, and one, called Cleopas, answered, 'Are you the only person staying in Jerusalem not to know what has happened there in the last few days?' 'What do you mean?' he said. 'All this about Jesus of Nazareth,' they replied, 'a prophet powerful in speech and action before God and the whole people; how our chief priests and rulers handed him over to be sentenced to death, and crucified him. But we had been hoping that he was the man to liberate Israel. What is more, this is the third day since it happened, and now some women of our company have astounded us: they went early to the tomb, but failed to find his body, and returned with a story that they had seen a vision of angels who told them he was alive. So some of our people went to the tomb and found things just as the women had said; but him they did not see.'

'How dull you are!' he answered. 'How slow to believe all that the prophets said! Was the Messiah not bound to suffer thus before entering upon his glory?' Then he began with Moses and all the prophets, and explained to them the passages which referred to himself in every part of the scriptures. By this time they had reached the village to which they were going, and he made as if to continue his journey, but they pressed him: 'Stay with us, for evening draws on, and the day is almost over.' So he went in to stay with them. And when he had sat down with them at table, he took bread and said the blessing; he broke the bread, and offered it to them. Then their eyes were opened, and they recognized him; and he vanished from their sight. They said to one another, 'Did we not feel our hearts on fire as he talked with us on the road and explained the scriptures to us?' **Luke 24: 13-32 NEB**

It was late that Sunday evening, and the disciples were gathered together behind locked doors, because they were afraid of the Jewish authorities. Then Jesus came and stood among them. "Peace be with you," he said. After saying this, he showed them his hands and his side. The disciples were filled with joy at seeing the Lord. Jesus said to them again, "Peace be with you. As the Father sent me, so I send you." Then he breathed on them and said, "Receive the Holy Spirit. If you forgive people's sins, they are forgiven; if you do not forgive them, they are not forgiven."

One of the twelve disciples, Thomas (called the Twin), was not with them when Jesus came. So the other disciples told him, "We have seen the Lord!" Thomas said to them, "Unless I see the scars of the nails in his hands and put my finger on those scars and my hand in his side, I will not believe." A week later the disciples were together again indoors, and Thomas was there with them. The doors were locked, but Jesus came and stood among them and said, "Peace be with you." Then he said to Thomas, "Put your finger here, and look at my hands; then reach out your hand and put it in my side. Stop your doubting and believe!" Thomas answered him, "My Lord and my God!" Jesus said to him, "Do you believe because you see me? How happy are those who believe without seeing me!" **John 20: 19-29 GNB~**

After this Jesus revealed himself again to the disciples by the Sea of Tiberias. Now this is how he did so. Simon Peter, Thomas (called Didymus), Nathanael (who was from Cana in Galilee), the sons of Zebedee, and two other disciples of his were together. Simon Peter told them, "I am going fishing." "We will go with you," they replied. They went out and got into the boat, but that night they caught nothing.

When it was already very early morning, Jesus stood on the beach, but the disciples did not know that it was Jesus. So Jesus said to them, "Children, you don't have any fish, do you?" They replied, "No." He told them, "Throw your net on the right side of the boat, and you will find some." So they threw the net, and were not able to pull it in because of the large number of fish.

Then the disciple whom Jesus loved said to Peter, "It is the Lord!"

So Simon Peter, when he heard that it was the Lord, tucked in his outer garment (for he had nothing on underneath it), and plunged into the sea. Meanwhile the other disciples came with the boat, dragging the net full of fish, for they were not far from land, only about a hundred yards. When they got out on the beach, they saw a charcoal fire ready with a fish placed on it, and bread. Jesus said, "Bring some of the fish you have just now caught."

So Simon Peter went aboard and pulled the net to shore. It was full of large fish, one hundred fifty-three, but although there were so many, the net was not torn. "Come, have breakfast," Jesus said. But none of the disciples dared to ask him, "Who are you?" because they knew it was the Lord. Jesus came and took the bread and gave it to them, and did the same with the fish. This was now the third time Jesus was revealed to the disciples after he was raised from the dead.

Then when they had finished breakfast, Jesus said to Simon Peter, "Simon, son of John, do you love me more than these do?" He replied, "Yes, Lord, you know I love you." Jesus told him, "Feed my lambs." Jesus said a second time, "Simon, son of John, do you love me?" He replied, "Yes, Lord, you know I love you." Jesus told him, "Shepherd my sheep." Jesus said a third time, "Simon, son of John, do you love me?" Peter was distressed that Jesus asked him a third time, "Do you love me?" and said, "Lord, you know everything. You know that I love you." Jesus replied, "Feed my sheep. I tell you the solemn truth, when you were young, you tied your clothes around you and went wherever you wanted, but when you are old, you will stretch out your hands, and others will tie you up and bring you where you do not want to go." (Now Jesus said this to indicate clearly by what kind of death Peter was going to glorify God.) After he said this, Jesus told Peter, "Follow me." **John 21: 1-19 NET**

So after talking with them the Lord Jesus was taken up into heaven, and he took his seat at the right hand of God; but they went out to make their proclamation everywhere, and the Lord worked with them and confirmed their words by the miracles that followed. **Mark 16: 19-20 NEB**

Jesus did many other miraculous signs in the presence of his disciples, which are not recorded in this book. But these are written that you may believe that Jesus is the Christ, the Son of God, and that by believing you may have life in his name. **John 20: 30-31 NIV**

"Men of Israel, hear these words: Jesus of Nazareth, a man attested to you by God with mighty works and wonders and signs which God did through him in your midst, as you yourselves know—this Jesus, delivered up according to the definite plan and foreknowledge of God, you crucified and killed by the hands of lawless men. But God raised him up, having loosed the pangs of death, because it was not possible for him to be held by it. For David says concerning him, 'I saw the Lord always before me, for he is at my right hand that I may not be shaken; therefore my heart was glad, and my tongue rejoiced; moreover my flesh will dwell in hope. For thou wilt not abandon my soul to Hades, nor let thy Holy One see corruption. Thou hast made known to me the ways of life; thou wilt make me full of gladness with thy presence.'

"Brethren, I may say to you confidently of the patriarch David that he both died and was buried, and his tomb is with us to this day. Being therefore a prophet, and knowing that God had sworn with an oath to him that he would set one of his descendants upon his throne, he foresaw and spoke of the resurrection of the Christ, that he was not abandoned to Hades, nor did his flesh see corruption. This Jesus God raised up, and of that we all are witnesses. Being therefore exalted at the right hand of God, and having received from the Father the promise of the Holy Spirit, he has poured out this which you see and hear. For David did not ascend into the heavens; but he himself says, 'The Lord said to my Lord, Sit at my right hand, till I make thy enemies a stool for thy feet.' Let all the house of Israel therefore know assuredly that God has made him both Lord and Christ, this Jesus whom you crucified." **Acts 2: 22-36 RSV**

Since the children have flesh and blood, he too shared in their humanity so that by his death he might destroy him who holds the power of death—that is, the devil—and free those who all their lives were held in slavery by their fear of death. For surely it is not angels he helps, but Abraham's descendants. For this reason he had to be made like his brothers in every way, in order that he might become a merciful and faithful high priest in service to God, and that he might make atonement for the sins of the people. Because he himself suffered when he was tempted, he is able to help those who are being tempted. **Hebrews 2: 14-18 NIV**

But now Christ has been raised from the dead, the firstfruits of those who have fallen asleep. For since death came through a man, the resurrection of the dead also came through a man. For just as in Adam all die, so also in Christ all will be made alive. But each in his own order: Christ, the firstfruits; then when Christ comes, those who belong to him.

Then comes the end, when he hands over the kingdom to God the Father, when he has brought to an end all rule and all authority and power. For he must reign until he has put all his enemies under his feet. The last enemy to be eliminated is death. For he has put everything in subjection under his feet. But when it says "everything" has been put in subjection, it is clear that this does not include the one who put everything in subjection to him. And when all things are subjected to him, then the Son himself will be subjected to the one who subjected everything to him, so that God may be all in all.

I Corinthians 15: 20-28 NET

The Holy Spirit

"I have yet many things to say to you, but you cannot bear them now. When the Spirit of truth comes, he will guide you into all the truth; for he will not speak on his own authority, but whatever he hears he will speak, and he will declare to you the things that are to come. He will glorify me, for he will take what is mine and declare it to you. All that the Father has is mine; therefore I said that he will take what is mine and declare it to you.
John 16: 12-15 RSV

Theophilus, in my first account, I wrote about all that Jesus said and did until he was taken up to heaven. Up to this time, he gave his apostles instructions through the power of the Holy Spirit. After his suffering and death, he also appeared to them many times, showing them convincingly that he was alive. They saw him and talked with him about the kingdom of God for over forty days. When they were all together he instructed them: "Do not leave Jerusalem until you receive the Holy Spirit—the gift promised by my Father. John

baptized with water, but soon you will be baptized with the Holy Spirit."
Acts 1: 1-5 HOV

When the day of Pentecost came, all the believers were gathered together in one place. Suddenly there was a noise from the sky which sounded like a strong wind blowing, and it filled the whole house where they were sitting. Then they saw what looked like tongues of fire which spread out and touched each person there. They were all filled with the Holy Spirit and began to talk in other languages, as the Spirit enabled them to speak.

There were Jews living in Jerusalem, religious men who had come from every country in the world. When they heard this noise, a large crowd gathered. They were all excited, because each one of them heard the believers talking in his own language. In amazement and wonder they exclaimed, "These people who are talking like this are Galileans! How is it, then, that all of us hear them speaking in our own native languages? We are from Parthia, Media, and Elam; from Mesopotamia, Judea, and Cappadocia; from Pontus and Asia, from Phrygia and Pamphylia, from Egypt and the regions of Libya near Cyrene. Some of us are from Rome, both Jews and Gentiles converted to Judaism, and some of us are from Crete and Arabia—yet all of us hear them speaking in our own languages about the great things that God has done!" Amazed and confused, they kept asking each other, "What does this mean?" But others made fun of the believers, saying, "These people are drunk!"

Then Peter stood up with the other eleven apostles and in a loud voice began to speak to the crowd: "Fellow Jews and all of you who live in Jerusalem, listen to me and let me tell you what this means. These people are not drunk, as you suppose; it is only nine o'clock in the morning. Instead, this is what the prophet Joel spoke about: 'This is what I will do in the last days, God says: I will pour out my Spirit on everyone. Your sons and daughters will proclaim my message; your young men will see visions, and your old men will have dreams. Yes, even on my servants, both men and women, I will pour out my Spirit in those days, and they will proclaim my message. I will perform miracles in the sky above and wonders on the earth below. There will be blood, fire, and thick smoke; the sun will be darkened, and the moon will turn red as blood, before the great and glorious Day of the Lord comes. And then, whoever calls out to the Lord for help will be saved.' **Acts 2: 1-21 GNB**

Now there was a man in Caesarea named Cornelius, a centurion of what was known as the Italian Cohort. He was a devout, God-fearing man, as was all his household; he did many acts of charity for the people and prayed to God regularly. About three o'clock one afternoon he saw clearly in a vision an angel of God who came in and said to him, "Cornelius." Staring at him and becoming greatly afraid, Cornelius replied, "What is it, Lord?" The angel said to him, "Your prayers and your acts of charity have gone up as a memorial before God. Now send men to Joppa and summon a man named Simon, who is called Peter. This man is staying as a guest with a man named Simon, a tanner, whose house is by the sea." When the angel who had spoken to him departed, Cornelius called two of his personal servants and a devout soldier from among those who served him, and when he had explained everything to them, he sent them to Joppa.

About noon the next day, while they were on their way and approaching the city, Peter went up on the roof to pray. He became hungry and wanted to eat, but while they were preparing the meal, a trance came over him. He saw heaven opened and an object something like a large sheet descending, being let down to earth by its four corners. In it were all kinds of four-footed animals and reptiles of the earth and wild birds. Then a voice said to him, "Get up, Peter; slaughter and eat!" But Peter said, "Certainly not, Lord, for I have never eaten anything defiled and ritually unclean!" The voice spoke to him again, a second time, "What God has made clean, you must not consider ritually unclean!" This happened three times, and immediately the object was taken up into heaven.

Now while Peter was puzzling over what the vision he had seen could signify, the men sent by Cornelius had learned where Simon's house was and approached the gate. They called out to ask if Simon, known as Peter, was staying there as a guest. While Peter was still thinking seriously about the vision, the Spirit said to him, "Look! Three men are looking for you. But get up, go down, and accompany them without hesitation, because I have sent them." So Peter went down to the men and said, "Here I am, the person you're looking for. Why have you come?" They said, "Cornelius the centurion, a righteous and God-fearing man, well spoken of by the whole Jewish nation, was directed by a holy angel to summon you to his house and to hear a message from you." So Peter invited them in and entertained them as guests.

On the next day he got up and set out with them, and some of the brothers from Joppa accompanied him. The following day he entered Caesarea. Now Cornelius was waiting anxiously for them and had called together his relatives and close friends. So when Peter came in, Cornelius met him, fell at his feet, and worshiped him. But Peter helped him up, saying, "Stand up. I too am a mere mortal." Peter continued talking with him as he went in, and he found many people gathered together. He said to them, "You know that it is unlawful for a Jew to associate with or visit a Gentile, yet God has shown me that I should call no person defiled or ritually unclean. Therefore when you sent for me, I came without any objection. Now may I ask why you sent for me?" Cornelius replied, "Four days ago at this very hour, at three o'clock in the afternoon, I was praying in my house, and suddenly a man in shining clothing stood before me and said, 'Cornelius, your prayer has been heard and your acts of charity have been remembered before God. Therefore send to Joppa and summon Simon, who is called Peter. This man is staying as a guest in the house of Simon the tanner, by the sea.' Therefore I sent for you at once, and you were kind enough to come. So now we are all here in the presence of God to listen to everything the Lord has commanded you to say to us."

Then Peter started speaking: "I now truly understand that God does not show favoritism in dealing with people, but in every nation the person who fears him and does what is right is welcomed before him. You know the message he sent to the people of Israel, proclaiming the good news of peace through Jesus Christ (he is Lord of all) –you know what happened throughout Judea, beginning from Galilee after the baptism that John announced: with respect to Jesus from Nazareth, that God anointed him with the Holy Spirit and with power. He went around doing good and healing all who were oppressed by the devil, because God was with him. We are witnesses of all the things he did both in Judea and in Jerusalem. They killed him by hanging him on a tree, but God raised him up on the third day and caused him to be seen, not by all the people, but by us, the witnesses God had already chosen, who ate and drank with him after he rose from the dead. He commanded us to preach to the people and to warn them that he is the one appointed by God as judge of the living and the dead. About him all the prophets testify, that everyone who believes in him receives forgiveness of sins through his name."

While Peter was still speaking these words, the Holy Spirit fell on all those who heard the message. The circumcised believers who had accompanied Peter were greatly astonished that the gift of the Holy Spirit had been poured out even on the Gentiles, for they heard them speaking in tongues and praising God. Then Peter said, "No one can withhold the water for these people to be baptized, who have received the Holy Spirit just as we did, can he?" So he gave orders to have them baptized in the name of Jesus Christ. Then they asked him to stay for several days. **Acts 10: 1-48 NET**

Those who are led by the Spirit of God are sons of God. For you did not receive a spirit that makes you a slave again to fear, but you received the Spirit of sonship. And by him we cry, "Abba, Father." The Spirit himself testifies with our spirit that we are God's children. Now if we are children, then we are heirs—heirs of God and co-heirs with Christ, if indeed we share in his sufferings in order that we may also share in his glory.
Romans 8: 14-17 NIV

For the Spirit explores everything, even the depths of God's own nature. Among men, who knows what a man is but the man's own spirit within him? In the

same way, only the Spirit of God knows what God is. This is the Spirit that we have received from God, and not the spirit of the world, so that we may know all that God of his own grace gives us; and, because we are interpreting spiritual truths to those who have the Spirit, we speak of these gifts of God in words found for us not by our human wisdom but by the Spirit. A man who is unspiritual refuses what belongs to the Spirit of God; it is folly to him; he cannot grasp it, because it needs to be judged in the light of the Spirit. A man gifted with the Spirit can judge the worth of everything, but is not himself subject to judgment by his fellow-men. For (in the words of Scripture) 'who knows the mind of the Lord? Who can advise him?' We, however, possess the mind of Christ.
I Corinthians 2: 10-16 NEB

Now about spiritual gifts, brothers, I do not want you to be ignorant. You know that when you were pagans, somehow or other you were influenced and led astray to mute idols. Therefore I tell you that no one who is speaking by the Spirit of God says, "Jesus be cursed," and no one can say, "Jesus is Lord," except by the Holy Spirit.

There are different kinds of gifts, but the same Spirit. There are different kinds of service, but the same Lord. There are different kinds of working, but the same God works all of them in all men. Now to each one the manifestation of the Spirit is given for the common good. To one there is given through the Spirit the message of wisdom, to another the message of knowledge by means of the same Spirit, to another faith by the same Spirit, to another gifts of healing by that one Spirit, to another miraculous powers, to another prophecy, to another distinguishing between spirits, to another speaking in different kinds of tongues, and to still another the interpretation of tongues. All these are the work of one and the same Spirit, and he gives them to each one, just as he determines. **I Corinthians 12: 1-11 NIV**

But I say, live by the Spirit and you will not carry out the desires of the flesh. For the flesh has desires that are opposed to the Spirit, and the Spirit has desires that are opposed to the flesh, for these are in opposition to each other, so that you cannot do what you want. But if you are led by the Spirit, you are not under the law. Now the works of the flesh are obvious: sexual immorality, impurity, depravity, idolatry, sorcery, hostilities, strife, jealousy, outbursts of anger, selfish rivalries, dissensions, factions, envying, murder, drunkenness, carousing, and similar things. I am warning you, as I had warned you before: Those who practice such things will not inherit the kingdom of God!

But the fruit of the Spirit is love, joy, peace, patience, kindness, goodness, faithfulness, gentleness, and self-control. Against such things there is no law. Now those who belong to Christ have crucified the flesh with its passions and desires. If we live by the Spirit, let us also behave in accordance with the Spirit. Let us not become conceited, provoking one another, being jealous of one another. **Galatians 5:16-26 NET**

SAUL IS CHANGED TO PAUL

And Saul approved of his (Stephen's) murder. That very day the church in Jerusalem began to suffer cruel persecution. All the believers, except the apostles, were scattered throughout the provinces of Judea and Samaria. Some devout men buried Stephen, mourning for him with loud cries. But Saul tried to destroy the church; going from house to house, he dragged out the believers, both men and women, and threw them into jail.
Acts 8: 1-3 GNB

But Saul, still breathing threats and murder against the disciples of the Lord, went to the high priest and asked him for letters to the synagogues at Damascus, so that if he found any belonging to the Way, men or women, he might bring them bound to Jerusalem. Now as he journeyed he approached Damascus, and suddenly a light from heaven flashed about him. And he fell to the ground and heard a voice saying to him, "Saul, Saul, why do you persecute me?" And he said, "Who are you, Lord?" And he said, "I am Jesus, whom you are persecuting; but rise and enter the city, and you will be told what you are to do." The men who were traveling with him stood speechless, hearing the voice but seeing no one. Saul arose from the ground; and when his eyes were opened, he could see nothing; so they led him by the hand and brought him into Damascus. And for three days he was without sight, and neither ate nor drank.

Now there was a disciple at Damascus named Ananias. The Lord said to him in a vision, "Ananias." And he said, "Here I am, Lord." And the Lord said to him, "Rise and go to the street called Straight, and inquire in the house of Judas for a man of Tarsus named Saul; for behold, he is praying, and he has seen a man named Ananias come in and lay his hands on him so that he might regain his sight." But Ananias answered, "Lord, I have heard from many about this man, how much evil he has done to thy saints at Jerusalem; and here he has authority from the chief priests to bind all who call upon thy name." But the Lord said to him, "Go, for he is a chosen instrument of mine to carry my name before the Gentiles and kings and the sons of Israel; for I will show him how much he must suffer for the sake of my name." So Ananias departed and entered the house. And laying his hands on him he said, "Brother Saul, the Lord Jesus who appeared to you on the road by which you came, has sent me that you may regain your sight and be filled with the Holy Spirit." And immediately something like scales fell from his eyes and he regained his sight. Then he rose and was baptized, and took food and was strengthened. **Acts 9: 1-19 RSV**

Saul spent several days with the disciples in Damascus. At once he began to preach in the synagogues that Jesus is the Son of God. All those who heard him were astonished and asked, "Isn't he the man who raised havoc in Jerusalem among those who call on this name? And hasn't he come here to take them as prisoners to the chief priests?" Yet Saul grew more and more powerful and baffled the Jews living in Damascus by proving that Jesus is the Christ. **Acts 9: 20-22 NIV**

Now after some days had passed, the Jews plotted together to kill him, but Saul learned of their plot against him. They were also watching the city gates day and night so that they could kill him. But his disciples took him at night and let him down through an opening in the wall by lowering him in a basket.

When he arrived in Jerusalem, he attempted to associate with the disciples, and they were all afraid of him, because they did not believe that he was a disciple. But Barnabas took Saul, brought him to the apostles, and related to them how he had seen the Lord on the road, that the Lord had spoken to him, and how in Damascus he had spoken out boldly in the name of Jesus. So he was staying with them, associating openly with them in Jerusalem, speaking out boldly in the name of the

Lord. He was speaking and debating with the Greek-speaking Jews, but they were trying to kill him. When the brothers found out about this, they brought him down to Caesarea and sent him away to Tarsus. **Acts 9: 23-30 NET**

I must make it clear to you, my friends, that the gospel you heard me preach is no human invention. I did not take it over from any man; no man taught me; I received it through a revelation of Jesus Christ.

You have heard what my manner of life was when I was still a practicing Jew: how savagely I persecuted the church of God, and tried to destroy it; and how in the practice of our national religion I was outstripping many of my Jewish contemporaries in my boundless devotion to the traditions of my ancestors. But then in his good pleasure God, who had set me apart from birth and called me through his grace, chose to reveal his Son to me and through me, in order that I might proclaim him among the Gentiles. When that happened, without consulting any human being, without going up to Jerusalem to see those who were apostles before me, I went off at once to Arabia, and afterwards returned to Damascus. Three years later I did go up to Jerusalem to get to know Cephas. I stayed with him for a fortnight, without seeing any other of the apostles, except James the Lord's brother. **Galatians 1: 11-19 NEB**

"Brothers and fathers, listen now to my defense." When they heard him speak to them in Aramaic, they became very quiet. Then Paul said: "I am a Jew, born in Tarsus of Cilicia, but brought up in this city. Under Gamaliel I was thoroughly trained in the law of our fathers and was just as zealous for God as any of you are today. I persecuted the followers of this Way to their death, arresting both men and women and throwing them into prison, as also the high priest and all the Council can testify. I even obtained letters from them to their brothers in Damascus, and went there to bring these people as prisoners to Jerusalem to be punished." **Acts 22: 1-5 NIV**

'After my return to Jerusalem, I was praying in the temple when I fell into a trance and saw him there, speaking to me. "Make haste", he said, "and leave Jerusalem without delay, for they will not accept your testimony about me." "Lord," I said, "they know that I imprisoned those who believe in thee, and flogged them in every synagogue; and when the blood of Stephen thy witness was shed I stood by, approving, and I looked after the clothes of those who killed him." But he said to me, "Go, for I am sending you far away to the Gentiles."'

Up to this point they had given him a hearing; but now they began shouting, 'Down with him! A scoundrel like that is better dead!' And as they were yelling and waving their cloaks and flinging dust in the air, the commandant ordered him to be brought into the barracks and gave instructions to examine him by flogging, and find out what reason there was for such an outcry against him. But when they tied him up for the lash, Paul said to the centurion who was standing there, "Can you legally flog a man who is a Roman citizen, and moreover has not been found guilty?' When the centurion heard this, he went and reported it to the commandant. 'What do you mean to do?' he said. 'This man is a Roman citizen.' The commandant came to Paul, 'Tell me, are you a Roman citizen?' he asked. 'Yes', said he. The commandant rejoined, 'It cost me a large sum to acquire this citizenship.' Paul said, 'But it was mine by birth.' Then those who were about to examine him withdrew hastily, and the commandant himself was alarmed when he realized that Paul was a Roman citizen and that he had put him in irons. **Acts 22: 22-29 NEB**

When we entered Rome, Paul was allowed to live by himself, with the soldier who was guarding him. After three days Paul called the local Jewish leaders together. When they had assembled, he said to them, "Brothers, although I had done nothing against our people or the customs of our ancestors, from Jerusalem I was handed over as a prisoner to the Romans. When they had heard my case, they wanted to release me, because there was no basis for a death sentence against me. But when the Jews objected, I was forced to appeal to Caesar – not that I had some charge to bring against my own people. So for this reason I have asked to see you and speak with you, for I am bound with this chain because of the hope of Israel." They replied, "We have received no letters from Judea about you, nor have any of the brothers come from there and reported or said anything bad about you. But we would like to hear from you what you think, for regarding this sect we know that people everywhere speak against it."

They set a day to meet with him, and they came to him where he was staying in even greater numbers. From morning until evening he explained things to them, testifying about the kingdom of God and trying to convince them about Jesus from both the law of Moses and the prophets. Some were convinced by what he said, but others refused to believe. So they began to leave, unable to agree among themselves, after Paul made one last statement: "The Holy Spirit spoke rightly to your ancestors through the prophet Isaiah when he said, 'Go to this people and say, "You will keep on hearing, but will never understand, and you will keep on looking, but will never perceive. For the heart of this people has become dull, and their ears are hard of hearing, and they have closed their eyes, so that they would not see with their eyes… and hear with their ears… and understand with their heart… and turn, and I would heal them."'

"Therefore be advised that this salvation from God has been sent to the Gentiles; they will listen!" Paul lived there two whole years in his own rented quarters and welcomed all who came to him, proclaiming the kingdom of God and teaching about the Lord Jesus Christ with complete boldness and without restriction. **Acts 28: 16-31 NET**

The Church The Body Of Christ

When the day of Pentecost came, all the believers were gathered together in one place. Suddenly there was a noise from the sky which sounded like a strong wind blowing, and it filled the whole house where they were sitting. Then they saw what looked like tongues of fire which spread out and touched each person there. They were all filled with the Holy Spirit and began to talk in other languages, as the Spirit enabled them to speak.
Acts 2: 1-4 GNB

When the people heard this, they were deeply troubled and said to Peter and the other apostles, "What shall we do, brothers?" Peter said to them, "Each one of you must turn away from his sins and be baptized in the name of Jesus Christ, so that your sins will be forgiven; and you will receive God's gift, the Holy Spirit. For God's promise was made to you and your children, and to all who are far away—all whom the Lord our God calls to himself."

Peter made his appeal to them and with many other words he urged them, saying, "Save yourselves from the punishment coming on this wicked people!" Many of them believed his message and were baptized, and about three thousand people were added to the group that day. They spent their time in learning from the apostles, taking part in the fellowship, and sharing in the fellowship meals and the prayers.

Many miracles and wonders were being done through the apostles, and everyone was filled with awe. All the believers continued together in close fellowship and shared their belongings with one another. They would sell their property and possessions, and distribute the money among all, according to what each one needed. Day after day they met as a group in the Temple, and they had their meals together in their homes, eating with glad and humble hearts, praising God, and enjoying the good will of all the people. And every day the Lord added to their group those who were being saved.
Acts 2: 37-47 GNB~

All the believers were one in heart and mind. No one claimed that any of his possessions was his own, but they shared everything they had. With great power the apostles continued to testify to the resurrection of the Lord Jesus, and much grace was upon them all.

There were no needy persons among them. For from time to time those who owned lands or houses sold them, brought the money from the sales and put it at the apostles' feet, and it was distributed to anyone as he had need.
Acts 4: 32-35 NIV

During this period, when disciples were growing in number, there was disagreement between those of them who spoke Greek and those who spoke the language of the Jews. The former party complained that their widows were being overlooked in the daily distribution. So the Twelve called the whole body of disciples together and said, 'It would be a grave mistake for us to neglect the word of God in order to wait at table. Therefore, friends, look out seven men of good reputation from your number, men full of the Spirit and of wisdom, and we will appoint them to deal with these matters, while we devote ourselves to prayer and to the ministry of the Word.' This proposal proved acceptable to the whole body. They elected Stephen, a man full of faith and of the Holy Spirit, Philip, Prochorus, Nicanor, Timon, Parmenas, and Nicolas of Antioch, a former convert to Judaism. These they presented to the apostles, who prayed and laid their hands on them. The word of God now spread more and more widely; the number of disciples in Jerusalem went on increasing rapidly, and very many of the priests adhered to the Faith. **Acts 6: 1-7 NEB**

Now in Joppa there was a disciple named Tabitha (which in translation means Dorcas). She was continually doing good deeds and acts of charity. At that time she became sick and died. When they had washed her body, they placed it in an upstairs room. Because Lydda was near Joppa, when the disciples heard that Peter was there, they sent two men to him and urged him, "Come to us without delay." So Peter got up and went with them, and when he arrived they brought him to the upper room. All the widows stood beside him, crying and showing him the tunics and other clothing Dorcas used to make while she was with them. But Peter sent them all outside, knelt down, and prayed. Turning to the body, he said, "Tabitha, get up." Then she opened her eyes, and when she saw Peter, she sat up. He gave her his hand and helped her get up. Then he called the saints and widows and presented her alive. This became known throughout all Joppa, and many believed in the Lord. So Peter stayed many days in Joppa with a man named Simon, a tanner.
Acts 9: 36-43 NET

Now those who had been scattered by the persecution in connection with Stephen traveled as far as Phoenicia, Cyprus and Antioch, telling the message only to Jews. Some of them, however, men from Cyprus and Cyrene, went to Antioch and began to speak to Greeks also, telling them the good news about the Lord Jesus. The Lord's hand was with them, and a great number of people believed and turned to the Lord. News of this reached the ears of the church at Jerusalem, and they sent Barnabas to Antioch. When he arrived and saw the evidence of the grace of God, he was glad and encouraged them all to remain true to the Lord with all their hearts. He was a good man, full of the Holy Spirit and faith, and a great number of people were brought to the Lord.

Then Barnabas went to Tarsus to look for Saul, and when he found him, he brought him to Antioch. So for a whole year Barnabas and Saul met with the church and taught great numbers of people. The disciples were called Christians first at Antioch. **Acts 11: 19-26 NIV**

In virtue of the gift that God in his grace has given me I say to everyone among you: do not be conceited or think too highly of yourself; but think your way to a sober estimate based on the measure of faith that God has dealt to each of you. For just as in a single human body there are many limbs and organs, all with different functions, so all of us, united with Christ, form one body, serving individually as limbs and organs to one another.

These gifts we possess differ as they are allotted to us by God's grace, and must be exercised accordingly: the gift of inspired utterance, for example, in proportion to a man's faith; or the gift of administration, in administration. A teacher should employ his gift in teaching, and one who has the gift of stirring speech should us it to stir his hearers. If you give to charity, give with all your heart; if you are a leader, exert yourself to lead; if you are helping others in distress, do it cheerfully.

Love in all sincerity, loathing evil and clinging to the good. Let love for our brotherhood breed warmth of mutual affection. Give pride of place to one another in esteem. With unflagging energy, in ardor of spirit, serve the Lord. Let hope keep you joyful; in trouble stand firm; persist in prayer. Contribute to the needs of God's people, and practice hospitality. Call down blessings on your persecutors—blessings, not curses. With the joyful be joyful, and mourn with the mourners. Have equal regard for one another. Do not be haughty, but go about with humble folk. Do not keep thinking how wise you are.

Never pay back evil for evil. Let your aims be such as all men count honorable. If possible, so far as it lies with you, live at peace with all men. My dear friends, do not seek revenge, but leave a place for divine retribution; for there is a text which reads, 'Justice is mine, says the Lord, I will repay.' But there is another text: 'If your enemy is hungry, feed him; if he is thirsty, give him a drink; by doing this you will heap live coals on his head.' Do not let evil conquer you, but use good to defeat evil. **Romans 12: 3-21 NEB~**

I appeal to you, brothers, in the name of our Lord Jesus Christ, that all of you agree with one another so that

there may be no divisions among you and that you may be perfectly united in mind and thought. My brothers, some from Chloe's household have informed me that there are quarrels among you. What I mean is this: One of you says, "I follow Paul"; another, "I follow Apollos"; another, "I follow Cephas"; still another, "I follow Christ." Is Christ divided? Was Paul crucified for you? Were you baptized into the name of Paul?
I Corinthians 1: 10-13 NIV

Christ didn't send me to baptize people, but to preach the gospel clearly and directly so that the cross of Christ would hold its rightful power. Preaching about Christ's death on the cross is nonsense to those caught up with evil, but to those being saved it's the power of God.
I Corinthians 1: 17-18 HOV

So then, my dear friends, keep away from the worship of idols. I speak to you as sensible people; judge for yourselves what I say. The cup we use in the Lord's Supper and for which we give thanks to God: when we drink from it, we are sharing in the blood of Christ. And the bread we break: when we eat it, we are sharing in the body of Christ. Because there is the one loaf of bread, all of us, though many, are one body, for we all share the same loaf. **I Corinthians 10: 14-17 GNB**

For just as the body is one and yet has many members, and all the members of the body – though many – are one body, so too is Christ. For in one Spirit we were all baptized into one body. Whether Jews or Greeks or slaves or free, we were all made to drink of the one Spirit. For in fact the body is not a single member, but many. If the foot says, "Since I am not a hand, I am not part of the body," it does not lose its membership in the body because of that. And if the ear says, "Since I am not an eye, I am not part of the body," it does not lose its membership in the body because of that. If the whole body were an eye, what part would do the hearing? If the whole were an ear, what part would exercise the sense of smell? But as a matter of fact, God has placed each of the members in the body just as he decided. If they were all the same member, where would the body be? So now there are many members, but one body. The eye cannot say to the hand, "I do not need you," nor in turn can the head say to the foot, "I do not need you." On the contrary, those members that seem to be weaker are essential, and those members we consider less honorable we clothe with greater honor, and our unpresentable members are clothed with dignity, but our presentable members do not need this. Instead, God has blended together the body, giving greater honor to the lesser member, so that there may be no division in the body, but the members may have mutual concern for one another. If one member suffers, everyone suffers with it. If a member is honored, all rejoice with it.

Now you are Christ's body, and each of you is a member of it. And God has placed in the church first apostles, second prophets, third teachers, then miracles, gifts of healing, helps, gifts of leadership, different kinds of tongues. Not all are apostles, are they? Not all are prophets, are they? Not all are teachers, are they? Not all perform miracles, do they? Not all have gifts of healing, do they? Not all speak in tongues, do they? Not all interpret, do they? But you should be eager for the greater gifts. **I Corinthians 12: 12-31 NET**

It was he who gave some to be apostles, some to be prophets, some to be evangelists, and some to be pastors and teachers, to prepare God's people for works of service, so that the body of Christ may be built up until we all reach unity in the faith and in the knowledge of the Son of God and become mature, attaining to the whole measure of the fullness of Christ.

Then we will no longer be infants, tossed back and forth by the waves, and blown here and there by every wind of teaching and by the cunning and craftiness of men in their deceitful scheming. Instead, speaking the truth in love, we will in all things grow up into him who is the Head, that is, Christ. From him the whole body, joined and held together by every supporting ligament, grows and builds itself up in love, as each part does its work. **Ephesians 4: 11-16 NIV**

Remember then your former condition: you, Gentiles as you are outwardly, you, 'the uncircumcised' so called by those who are called 'the circumcised' (but only with reference to an outward rite)—you were at that time separate from Christ, strangers to the community of Israel, outside God's covenants and the promise that goes with them. Your world was a world without hope and without God. But now in union with Christ Jesus you who once were far off have been brought near through the shedding of Christ's blood. For he is himself our peace. Gentiles and Jews, he has made the two one, and in his own body of flesh and blood has broken down the enmity which stood like a dividing wall between them; for he annulled the law with its rules and regulations, so as to create out of the two a single new humanity in himself, thereby making peace. This was his purpose, to reconcile the two in a single body to God through the cross, on which he killed the enmity.

So he came and proclaimed the good news: peace to you who were far off, and peace to those who were near by; for through him we both alike have access to the Father in the one Spirit. Thus you are no longer aliens in a foreign land, but fellow-citizens with God's people, members of God's household. You are built upon the foundation laid by the apostles and prophets, and Christ Jesus himself is the foundation-stone. In him the whole building is bonded together and grows into a holy temple in the Lord. In him you too are being built with all the rest into a spiritual dwelling for God.
Ephesians 2: 11-22 NEB

I, therefore, the prisoner for the Lord, urge you to live worthily of the calling with which you have been called, with all humility and gentleness, with patience, bearing with one another in love, making every effort to keep the unity of the Spirit in the bond of peace. There is one body and one Spirit, just as you too were called to the one hope of your calling, one Lord, one faith, one baptism, one God and Father of all, who is over all and through all and in all. **Ephesians 4: 1-6 NET~**

God's plan is to make known his secret to his people, this rich and glorious secret which he has for all peoples. And the secret is that Christ is in you, which means that you will share in the glory of God. So we preach Christ to everyone. With all possible wisdom we warn and teach them in order to bring each one into God's presence as a mature individual in union with Christ. **Colossians 1: 27-29 GNB**

The Law

Blessed is the man who walks not in the counsel of the wicked, nor stands in the way of sinners, nor sits in the seat of scoffers; but his delight is in the law of the Lord, and on his law he meditates day and night. He is like a tree planted by streams of water, that yields its fruit in its season, and its leaf does not wither. In all that he does, he prospers. The wicked are not so, but are like chaff which the wind drives away. Therefore the wicked will not stand in the judgment, nor sinners in the congregation of the righteous; for the Lord knows the way of the righteous, but the way of the wicked will perish.
Psalms 1: 1-6 RSV

Stephen answered, "Brothers and fathers, listen to me! Before our ancestor Abraham had gone to live in Haran, the God of glory appeared to him in Mesopotamia and said to him, 'Leave your family and country and go to the land that I will show you.' And so he left his country and went to live in Haran. After Abraham's father died, God made him move to this land where you now live. God did not then give Abraham any part of it as his own, not even a square foot of ground, but God promised to give it to him, and that it would belong to him and to his descendants. At the time God made this promise, Abraham had no children. This is what God said to him: 'Your descendants will live in a foreign country, where they will be slaves and will be badly treated for four hundred years. But I will pass judgment on the people that they will serve, and afterward they will come out of that country and will worship me in this place.' Then God gave to Abraham the ceremony of circumcision as a sign of the covenant. So Abraham circumcised Isaac a week after he was born; Isaac circumcised his son Jacob, and Jacob circumcised his twelve sons, the famous ancestors of our race.

"Jacob's sons became jealous of their brother Joseph and sold him to be a slave in Egypt. But God was with him and brought him safely through all his troubles. When Joseph appeared before the king of Egypt, God gave him a pleasing manner and wisdom, and the king made Joseph governor over the country and the royal household. Then there was a famine all over Egypt and Canaan, which caused much suffering. Our ancestors could not find any food, and when Jacob heard that there was grain in Egypt, he sent his sons, our ancestors, on their first visit there. On the second visit Joseph made himself known to his brothers, and the king of Egypt came to know about Joseph's family. So Joseph sent a message to his father Jacob, telling him and the whole family, seventy-five people in all, to come to Egypt. Then Jacob went to Egypt, where he and his sons died. Their bodies were taken to Shechem, where they were buried in the grave which Abraham had bought from the clan of Hamor for a sum of money.

"When the time drew near for God to keep the promise he had made to Abraham, the number of our people in Egypt had grown much larger. At last a king who did not know about Joseph began to rule in Egypt. He tricked our ancestors and was cruel to them, forcing them to put their babies out of their homes, so that they would die. It was at this time that Moses was born, a very beautiful child. He was cared for at home for three months, and when he was put out of his home, the king's daughter adopted him and brought him up as her own son. He was taught all the wisdom of the Egyptians and became a great man in words and deeds.

"When Moses was forty years old, he decided to find out how his fellow Israelites were being treated. He saw one of them being mistreated by an Egyptian, so he went to his help and took revenge on the Egyptian by killing him. (He thought that his own people would understand that God was going to use him to set them free, but they did not understand.) The next day he saw two Israelites fighting, and he tried to make peace between them. 'Listen, men,' he said 'you are fellow Israelites; why are you fighting like this?' But the one who was mistreating the other pushed Moses aside.

'Who made you ruler and judge over us?' he asked. 'Do you want to kill me, just as you killed that Egyptian yesterday?' When Moses heard this, he fled from Egypt and went to live in the land of Midian. There he had two sons.

"After forty years had passed, an angel appeared to Moses in the flames of a burning bush in the desert near Mount Sinai. Moses was amazed by what he saw, and went near the bush to get a better look. But he heard the Lord's voice: 'I am the God of your ancestors, the God of Abraham, Isaac, and Jacob.' Moses trembled with fear and dared not look. The Lord said to him, 'Take your sandals off, for the place where you are standing is holy ground. I have seen the cruel suffering of my people in Egypt. I have heard their groans, and I have come down to set them free. Come now; I will send you to Egypt.'

"Moses is the one who was rejected by the people of Israel. 'Who made you ruler and judge over us?' they asked. He is the one whom God sent to rule the people and set them free with the help of the angel who appeared to him in the burning bush. He led the people out of Egypt, performing miracles and wonders in Egypt and at the Red Sea and for forty years in the desert. Moses is the one who said to the people of Israel, 'God will send you a prophet, just as he sent me, and he will be one of your own people. He is the one who was with the people of Israel assembled in the desert;

he was there with our ancestors and with the angel who spoke to him on Mount Sinai, and he received God's living messages to pass on to us.

"But our ancestors refused to obey him; they pushed him aside and wished that they could go back to Egypt. So they said to Aaron, 'Make us some gods who will lead us. We do not know what has happened to that man Moses, who brought us out of Egypt.' It was then that they made an idol in the shape of a bull, offered sacrifice to it, and had a feast in honor of what they themselves had made. So God turned away from them and gave them over to worship the stars of heaven, as it is written in the book of the prophets: 'People of Israel! It was not to me that you slaughtered and sacrificed animals for forty years in the desert. It was the tent of the god Molech that you carried, and the image of Rephan, your star god; they were idols that you had made to worship. And so I will send you into exile beyond Babylon.'

"Our ancestors had the Covenant Tent with them in the desert. It had been made as God had told Moses to make it, according to the pattern that Moses had been shown. Later on, our ancestors who received the tent from their fathers carried it with them when they went with Joshua and took over the land from the nations that God drove out as they advanced. And it stayed there until the time of David. He won God's favor and asked God to allow him to provide a dwelling place for the God of Jacob. But it was Solomon who built him a house. "But the Most High God does not live in houses built by men; as the prophet says, 'Heaven is my throne, says the Lord, and earth is my footstool. What kind of house would you build for me? Where is the place for me to live in? Did not I myself make all these things?' "How stubborn you are!" Stephen went on to say. "How heathen your hearts, how deaf you are to God's message! You are just like your ancestors: you too have always resisted the Holy Spirit! Was there any prophet that your ancestors did not persecute? They killed God's messengers, who long ago announced the coming of his righteous Servant. And now you have betrayed and murdered him. You are the ones who received God's law, that was handed down by angels—yet you have not obeyed it!" **Acts 7: 2-53 GNB**

"Do not think that I have come to abolish the Law or the Prophets; I have not come to abolish them but to fulfill them. I tell you the truth, until heaven and earth disappear, not the smallest letter, not the least stroke of a pen, will by any means disappear from the Law until everything is accomplished. Anyone who breaks one of the least of these commandments and teaches others to do the same will be called least in the kingdom of heaven, but whoever practices and teaches these commands will be called great in the kingdom of heaven. For I tell you that unless your righteousness surpasses that of the Pharisees and the teachers of the law, you will certainly not enter the kingdom of heaven. **Matthew 5: 17-20 NIV**

Jesus was walking through some wheat fields on a Sabbath. As his disciples walked along with him, they began to pick the heads of wheat. So the Pharisees said to Jesus, "Look, it is against our Law for your disciples to do that on the Sabbath!" Jesus answered, "Have you never read what David did that time when he needed something to eat? He and his men were hungry, so he went into the house of God and ate the bread offered to God. This happened when Abiathar was the High Priest. According to our Law only the priests may eat this bread—but David ate it and even gave it to his men." And Jesus concluded, "The Sabbath was made for the good of man; man was not made for the Sabbath. So the Son of Man is Lord even of the Sabbath." **Mark 2: 23-28 GNB**

For God has no favorites: those who have sinned outside the pale of the Law of Moses will perish outside its pale, and all who have sinned under that law will be judged by the law. It is not by hearing the law, but by doing it, that men will be justified before God. When Gentiles who do not possess the law carry out its precepts by the light of nature, then, although they have no law, they are their own law, for they display the effect of the law inscribed on their hearts. Their conscience is called as witness and their own thoughts argue the case on either side, against them or even for them, on the day when God judges the secrets of human hearts through Christ Jesus. So my gospel declares.

But as for you—you may bear the name of Jew; you rely upon the law and are proud of your God; you know his will; you are aware of moral distinctions because you receive instruction from the law; you are confident that you are the one to guide the blind, to enlighten the benighted, to train the stupid, and to teach the immature, because in the law you see the very shape of knowledge and truth. You, then, who teach your fellow-man, do you fail to teach yourself? You proclaim, 'Do not steal'; but are you yourself a thief? You say, 'Do not commit adultery'; but are you an adulterer? You abominate false gods; but do you rob their shrines? While you take pride in the law, you dishonor God by breaking it. For, as Scripture says, 'Because of you the name of God is dishonored among the Gentiles.'

Circumcision has value, provided you keep the law; but if you break the law, then your circumcision is as if it had never been. Equally, if an uncircumcised man keeps the precepts of the law, will he not count as circumcised? He may be uncircumcised in his natural state, but by fulfilling the law he will pass judgment on you who break it, for all your written code and your circumcision. The true Jew is not he who is such in externals, neither is the true circumcision the external mark in the flesh. The true Jew is he who is such inwardly, and the true circumcision is of the heart, directed not by written precepts but by the Spirit; such a man receives his commendation not from men but from God. **Romans 2: 11-29 NEB**

Now we know that everything in the Law applies to those who live under the Law, in order to stop all human excuses and bring the whole world under God's judgment. For no one is put right in God's sight by doing what the Law requires; what the Law does is to make man know that he has sinned. **Romans 3: 19-20 GNB**

Mark what follows. It was through one man that sin entered the world, and through sin death, and thus death pervaded the whole human race, inasmuch as all men have sinned. For sin was already in the world before there was law, though in the absence of law no reckoning is kept of sin. But death held sway from Adam to Moses, even over those who had not sinned as Adam did, by disobeying a direct command—and Adam foreshadows the Man who was to come. **Romans 5: 12-14 NEB**

JUDGMENT

The LORD God took the man and put him in the Garden of Eden to work it and take care of it. And the LORD God commanded the man, "You are free to eat from any tree in the garden; but you must not eat from the tree of the knowledge of good and evil, for when you eat of it you will surely die." **Genesis 2: 15-17 NIV**

This is what the LORD says: "For three sins of Israel, even for four, I will not turn back {my wrath}. They sell the righteous for silver, and the needy for a pair of sandals. They trample on the heads of the poor as upon the dust of the ground and deny justice to the oppressed. Father and son use the same girl and so profane my holy name. They lie down beside every altar on garments taken in pledge. In the house of their god they drink wine taken as fines. **Amos 2: 6-8 NIV**

Woe to you who are complacent in Zion, and to you who feel secure on Mount Samaria, you notable men of the foremost nation, to whom the people of Israel come! Go to Calneh and look at it; go from there to great

Hamath, and then go down to Gath in Philistia. Are they better off than your two kingdoms? Is their land larger than yours? You put off the evil day and bring near a reign of terror. You lie on beds inlaid with ivory and lounge on your couches. You dine on choice lambs and fattened calves. You strum away on your harps like David and improvise on musical instruments. You drink wine by the bowlful and use the finest lotions, but you do not grieve over the ruin of Joseph. Therefore you will be among the first to go into exile; your feasting and lounging will end. **Amos 6: 1-7 NIV**

Hear this, you who trample the needy and do away with the poor of the land, saying, "When will the New Moon be over that we may sell grain, and the Sabbath be ended that we may market wheat?"—skimping the measure, boosting the price and cheating with dishonest scales, buying the poor with silver and the needy for a pair of sandals, selling even the sweepings with the wheat. The LORD has sworn by the Pride of Jacob: "I will never forget anything they have done." **Amos 8: 4-7 NIV**

Yet they sinned still more against him, rebelling against the Most High in the desert. They tested God in their heart by demanding the food they craved. They spoke against God, saying, "Can God spread a table in the wilderness? He smote the rock so that water gushed out and steams overflowed. Can he also give bread, or provide meat for his people?" Therefore, when the Lord heard, he was full of wrath; a fire was kindled against

Jacob, his anger mounted against Israel; because they had no faith in God, and did not trust his saving power. Yet he commanded the skies above, and opened the doors of heaven; and he rained down upon them manna to eat, and gave them the grain of heaven. Man ate of the bread of angels; he sent them food in abundance. He caused the east wind to blow in the heavens, and by his power he led out the south wind; he rained flesh upon them like dust, winged birds like the sand of the seas; he let them fall in the midst of their camp, all around their habitations. And they ate and were filled, for he gave them what they craved. But before they had sated their craving, while the food was still in their mouths, the anger of God rose against them and he slew the strongest of them, and laid low the picked men of Israel. **Psalms 78: 17-31 RSV**

The LORD takes his place in court; he rises to judge the people. The LORD enters into judgment against the elders and leaders of his people: "It is you who have ruined my vineyard; the plunder from the poor is in your houses. What do you mean by crushing my people and grinding the faces of the poor?" declares the Lord, the LORD Almighty. **Isaiah 3: 13-15 NIV**

Woe to you who add house to house and join field to field till no space is left and you live alone in the land. The LORD Almighty has declared in my hearing: "Surely the great houses will become desolate, the fine mansions left without occupants. A ten-acre vineyard will produce only a bath of wine, a homer of seed only an ephah of grain." Woe to those who rise early in the morning to run after their drinks, who stay up late at night till they are inflamed with wine. They have harps and lyres at their banquets, tambourines and flutes and wine, but they have no regard for the deeds of the LORD, no respect for the work of his hands. **Isaiah 5: 8-12 NIV**

"Therefore, thus says the Lord God to them: Behold, I, I myself will judge between the fat sheep and the lean sheep. Because you push with side and shoulder, and thrust at all the weak with your horns, till you have scattered them abroad, I will save my flock, they shall no longer be a prey; and I will judge between sheep and sheep. And I will set up over them one shepherd, my servant David, and he shall feed them: he shall feed them and be their shepherd. And I, the Lord, will be their God, and my servant David shall be prince among them; I, the Lord, have spoken. **Ezekiel 34: 20-24 RSV**

"I did not say these things to you from the beginning, because I was with you. But now I am going to him who sent me; yet none of you asks me, 'Where are you going?' But because I have said these things to you, sorrow has filled your hearts. Nevertheless I tell you the truth: it is to your advantage that I go away, for if I do not go away, the Counselor will not come to you; but if I go, I will send him to you. And when he comes, he will convince the world of sin and of righteousness and of judgment: of sin, because they do not believe in me; of righteousness, because I go to the Father, and you will see me no more; of judgment, because the ruler of this world is judged. **John 16: 4-11 RSV**

"For the kingdom of heaven is like a landowner who went out early in the morning to hire workers for his vineyard. And after agreeing with the workers for the standard wage, he sent them into his vineyard. When it was about nine o'clock in the morning, he went out again and saw others standing around in the marketplace without work. He said to them, 'You go into the vineyard too, and I will give you whatever is right.' So they went. When he went out again about noon and three o'clock that afternoon, he did the same thing. And about five o'clock that afternoon he went out and found others standing around, and said to them, 'Why are you standing here all day without work?' They said to him, 'Because no one hired us.' He said to them, 'You go and work in the vineyard too.'

When it was evening the owner of the vineyard said to his manager, 'Call the workers and give the pay starting with the last hired until the first.' When those hired about five o'clock came, each received a full day's pay. And when those hired first came, they thought they would receive more. But each one also received the standard wage. When they received it, they began to complain against the landowner, saying, 'These last fellows worked one hour, and you have made them equal

to us who bore the hardship and burning heat of the day.' And the landowner replied to one of them, 'Friend, I am not treating you unfairly. Didn't you agree with me to work for the standard wage? Take what is yours and go. I want to give to this last man the same as I gave to you. Am I not permitted to do what I want with what belongs to me? Or are you envious because I am generous?' So the last will be first, and the first last."
Matthew 20: 1-16 NET

He also said to them, "Pay attention to what you hear! The same rules you use to judge others will be used by God to judge you—but with even greater severity.
Mark 4: 24 GNB

So then, men ought to regard us as servants of Christ and as those entrusted with the secret things of God. Now it is required that those who have been given a trust must prove faithful. I care very little if I am judged by you or by any human court; indeed, I do not even judge myself. My conscience is clear, but that does not make me innocent. It is the Lord who judges me. Therefore judge nothing before the appointed time; wait till the Lord comes. He will bring to light what is hidden in darkness and will expose the motives of men's hearts. At that time each will receive his praise from God.
I Corinthians 4: 1-5 NIV

Then everyone went home, but Jesus went to the Mount of Olives. Early the next morning he went back to the

Temple. All of the people gathered around him, and he sat down and began to teach them. The teachers of the Law and the Pharisees brought in a woman who had been caught committing adultery, and they made her stand before them all. "Teacher," they said to Jesus, "this woman was caught in the very act of committing adultery. In our Law Moses commanded that such a woman must be stoned to death. Now, what do you say?" They said this to trap Jesus, so that they could accuse him. But he bent over and wrote on the ground with his finger. As they stood there asking him questions, he straightened up and said to them, "Whichever one of you has committed no sin may throw the first stone at her." Then he bent over again and wrote on the ground. When they heard this, they all left, one by one, the older ones first. Jesus was left alone, with the woman still standing there. He straightened up and said to her, "Where are they? Is there no one left to condemn you?" "No one, sir," she answered. "Well, then," Jesus said, "I do not condemn you either. Go, but do not sin again."
John 8: 1-11 GNB

"No one after lighting a lamp puts it in a hidden place or under a basket, but on a lampstand, so that those who come in can see the light. Your eye is the lamp of your body. When your eye is healthy, your whole body is full of light, but when it is diseased, your body is full of darkness. Therefore see to it that the light in you is not darkness. If then your whole body is full of light, with no part in the dark, it will be as full of light as when the light of a lamp shines on you."

As he spoke, a Pharisee invited Jesus to have a meal with him, so he went in and took his place at the table. The Pharisee was astonished when he saw that Jesus did not first wash his hands before the meal. But the Lord said to him, "Now you Pharisees clean the outside of the cup and the plate, but inside you are full of greed and wickedness. You fools! Didn't the one who made the outside make the inside as well? But give from your heart to those in need, and then everything will be clean for you.

"But woe to you Pharisees! You give a tenth of your mint, rue, and every herb, yet you neglect justice and love for God! But you should have done these things without neglecting the others. Woe to you Pharisees! You love the best seats in the synagogues and elaborate greetings in the marketplaces! Woe to you! You are like unmarked graves, and people walk over them without realizing it!"
Luke 11: 33-44 NET

"The kingdom of heaven is like this. Once there was a king who prepared a wedding feast for his son. He sent his servants to tell the invited guests to come to the feast, but they did not want to come. Se he sent other servants with this message for the guests: 'My feast is ready now; my steers and prize calves have been butchered, and everything is ready. Come to the wedding feast!' But the invited guests paid no attention and went about their business: one went to his farm, another to his store, while others grabbed the servants, beat them, and killed them. The king was very angry; so he sent soldiers, who killed those murderers and burned down their city. Then he called his servants and said to them, 'My wedding feast is ready, but the people I invited did not deserve it. Now go to the main streets and invite to the feast as many people as you find.' So the servants went out into the streets and gathered all the people they could find, good and bad alike; and the wedding hall was filled with people.

The king went in to look at the guests and saw a man who was not wearing wedding clothes. 'Friend, how did you get in here without wedding clothes?' the king asked him. But the man said nothing. Then the king told the servants, 'Tie him up hand and foot, and throw him outside in the dark. There he will cry and gnash his teeth.'" And Jesus concluded, "Many are invited, but few are chosen." **Matthew 22: 2-14 GNB**

"At that time the kingdom of heaven will be like ten virgins who took their lamps and went out to meet the bridegroom. Five of them were foolish and five were wise. The foolish ones took their lamps but did not take any oil with them. The wise, however, took oil in jars along with their lamps. The bridegroom was a long time in coming, and they all became drowsy and fell asleep. At midnight the cry rang out: 'Here's the bridegroom! Come out to meet him!' Then all the virgins woke up and trimmed their lamps. The foolish ones said to the wise, 'Give us some of your oil; our lamps are going out.' 'No,' they replied, 'there may not be enough for both us and you. Instead, go to those who sell oil and buy some for yourselves.' But while they were on their way to buy the oil, the bridegroom arrived. The virgins who were ready went in with him to the wedding banquet. And the door was shut. Later the others also came. 'Sir! Sir!' they said. 'Open the door for us!' But he replied, 'I tell you the truth, I don't know you.' Therefore keep watch, because you do not know the day or the hour." **Matthew 25: 1-13 NIV**

No one knows, however, when that day and hour will come—neither the angels in heaven nor the Son; the Father alone knows. The coming of the Son of Man will be like what happened in the time of Noah. In the days before the flood people ate and drank, men and women married, up to the very day Noah went into the boat; yet they did not realize what was happening until the flood came and swept them all away. That is how it will be when the Son of Man comes. At that time two men will be working in a field: one will be taken away, the other will be left behind. Two women will be at a mill grinding meal: one will be taken away, the other will be left behind. Watch out, then, because you do not know what day your Lord will come. If the owner of a house knew the time when the thief would come, you can be sure that he would stay awake and not let the thief break into his house. So then, you also must always be ready, because the Son of Man will come at an hour when you are not expecting him. **Matthew 24: 36-44 GNB**

"When the Son of man comes in his glory, and all the angels with him, then he will sit on his glorious throne. Before him will be gathered all the nations, and he will separate them one from another as a shepherd separates the sheep from the goats, and he will place the sheep at his right hand, but the goats at the left. Then the King will say to those at his right hand, 'Come, O blessed of my Father, inherit the kingdom prepared for you from the foundation of the world; for I was hungry and you gave me food, I was thirsty and you gave me drink, I was a stranger and you welcomed me, I was naked and you clothed me, I was sick and you visited me, I was in prison and you came to me.' Then the righteous will answer him, 'Lord, when did we see thee hungry and feed thee, or thirsty and give thee drink? And when did we see thee a stranger and welcome thee, or naked and clothe thee? And when did we see thee sick or in prison and visit thee? And the King will answer them, 'Truly, I say to you, as you did it to one of the least of these my brethren, you did it to me.' Then he will say to those at his left hand, 'Depart from me, you cursed, into the eternal fire prepared for the devil and his angels; for I was hungry and you gave me no food, I was thirsty and you gave me no drink, I was a stranger and you did not welcome me, naked and you did not clothe me, sick and in prison and you did not visit me.' Then they also will answer, 'Lord, when did we see thee hungry or thirsty or a stranger or naked or sick or in prison, and did not minister to thee?' Then he will answer them, 'Truly, I say to you, as you did it not to one of the least of these, you did it not to me.' And they will go away into eternal punishment, but the righteous into eternal life." **Matthew 25: 31-46 RSV***

"But woe to you who are rich, for you have already received your comfort. Woe to you who are well fed now, for you will go hungry. Woe to you who laugh now, for you will mourn and weep. Woe to you when all men speak well of you, for that is how their fathers treated the false prophets." **Luke 6: 24-26 NIV**

You therefore have no defense—you who sit in judgment, whoever you may be—for in judging your fellow-man you condemn yourself, since you, the judge, are equally guilty. It is admitted that God's judgment is rightly passed upon all who commit such crimes as these; and do you imagine—you who pass judgment on the guilty while committing the same crimes yourself—do you imagine that you, any more than they, will escape the judgment of God? Or do you think lightly of his wealth of kindness, of tolerance, and of patience, without recognizing that God's kindness is meant to lead you to a change of heart? In the rigid obstinacy of your heart you are laying up for yourself a store of

retribution for the day of retribution, when God's just judgment will be revealed, and he will pay every man for what he has done. To those who pursue glory, honor, and immortality by steady persistence in well-doing, he will give eternal life; but for those who are governed by selfish ambition, who refuse obedience to the truth and take the wrong for their guide, there will be the fury of retribution. There will be grinding misery for every human being who is an evil-doer, for the Jew first and for the Greek also; and for every well-doer there will be glory, honor, and peace, for the Jew first and also for the Greek.
Romans 2: 1-10 NEB

All this is evidence that God's judgment is right, and as a result you will be counted worthy of the kingdom of God, for which you are suffering. God is just: He will pay back trouble to those who trouble you and give relief to you who are troubled, and to us as well. This will happen when the Lord Jesus is revealed from heaven in blazing fire with his powerful angels. He will punish those who do not know God and do not obey the gospel of our Lord Jesus. They will be punished with everlasting destruction and shut out from the presence of the Lord and from the majesty of his power on the day he comes to be glorified in his holy people and to be marveled at among all those who have believed. This includes you, because you believed our testimony to you.
II Thessalonians 1: 5-10 NIV

JUSTICE

For the Lord your God is God of gods and Lord of lords, the great, the mighty, and the terrible God, who is not partial and takes no bribe. He executes justice for the fatherless and the widow, and loves the sojourner, giving him food and clothing. Love the sojourner therefore; for you were sojourners in the land of Egypt. You shall fear the Lord your God; you shall serve him and cleave to him, and by his name you shall swear.
Deuteronomy 10: 17-20 RSV

Do not deprive the alien or the fatherless of justice, or take the cloak of the widow as a pledge. Remember that you were slaves in Egypt and the LORD your God redeemed you from there. That is why I command you to do this. **Deuteronomy 24: 17-18 NIV**

Endow the king with your justice, O God, the royal son with your righteousness. He will judge your people in righteousness, your afflicted ones with justice. The mountains will bring prosperity to the people, the hills the fruit of righteousness. He will defend the afflicted among the people and save the children of the needy; he will crush the oppressor. **Psalms 72: 1-4 NIV**

"Is not this the fast that I choose: to loose the bonds of wickedness, to undo the thongs of the yoke, to let the oppressed go free, and to break every yoke? Is it not to share your bread with the hungry, and bring the homeless poor into your house; when you see the naked, to cover him, and not to hide yourself from your own flesh? Then shall your light break forth like the dawn, and your healing shall spring up speedily; your righteousness shall go before you, the glory of the Lord shall be your rear guard.

Then you shall call, and the Lord will answer; you shall cry, and he will say, Here I am. "If you take away from the midst of you the yoke, the pointing of the finger, and speaking wickedness, if you pour yourself out for the hungry and satisfy the desire of the afflicted, then shall your light rise in the darkness and your gloom be as the noonday. And the Lord will guide you continually, and satisfy your desire with good things, and make your bones strong; and you shall be like a watered garden, like a spring of water, whose waters fail not. And your ancient ruins shall be rebuilt; you shall raise up the foundations of many generations; you shall be called the repairer of the breach, the restorer of streets to dwell in. **Isaiah 58: 6-11 RSV**

For I know how many are your transgressions, and

how great are your sins—you who afflict the righteous, who take a bribe, and turn aside the needy in the gate. Therefore he who is prudent will keep silent in such a time; for it is an evil time. Seek good, and not evil, that you may live; and so the Lord, the God of hosts, will be with you, as you have said. Hate evil, and love good, and establish justice in the gate; it may be that the Lord, the God of hosts, will be gracious to the remnant of Joseph. **Amos 5: 12-15 RSV**

"I hate, I despise your feasts, and I take no delight in your solemn assemblies. Even though you offer me your burnt offerings and cereal offerings, I will not accept them, and the peace offerings of your fatted beasts I will not look upon. Take away from me the noise of your songs; to the melody of your harps I will not listen. But let justice roll down like waters, and righteousness like an ever-flowing stream. **Amos 5: 21-24 RSV**

"There was a rich man who dressed in purple and fine linen and who feasted sumptuously every day. But at his gate lay a poor man named Lazarus whose body was covered with sores, who longed to eat what fell from the rich man's table. In addition, the dogs came and licked his sores.

"Now the poor man died and was carried by the angels to Abraham's side. The rich man also died and was buried. And in hell, as he was in torment, he looked up and saw Abraham far off with Lazarus at his side.

So he called out, 'Father Abraham, have mercy on me, and send Lazarus to dip the tip of his finger in water and cool my tongue, because I am in anguish in this fire.' But Abraham said, 'Child, remember that in your lifetime you received your good things and Lazarus likewise bad things, but now he is comforted here and you are in anguish. Besides all this, a great chasm has been fixed between us, so that those who want to cross over from here to you cannot do so, and no one can cross from there to us.' So the rich man said, 'Then I beg you, father – send Lazarus to my father's house (for I have five brothers) to warn them so that they don't come into this place of torment.' But Abraham said, 'They have Moses and the prophets; they must respond to them.' Then the rich man said, 'No, father Abraham, but if someone from the dead goes to them, they will repent.' He replied to him, 'If they do not respond to Moses and the prophets, they will not be convinced even if someone rises from the dead.'" **Luke 16: 19-31 NET+**

But now, quite independently of law, God's justice has been brought to light. The Law and the prophets both bear witness to it: it is God's way of righting wrong effective through faith in Christ for all who have such faith—all, without distinction. For all alike have sinned, and are deprived of the divine splendor, and all are justified by God's free grace alone, through his act of liberation in the person of Christ Jesus. For God designed him to be the means of expiating sin by his sacrificial death, effective through faith. God meant by this to demonstrate his justice, because in his forbearance he had overlooked the sins of the past—to demonstrate his justice now in the present, showing that he is both himself just and justifies any man who puts his faith in Jesus.

What room then is left for human pride? It is excluded. And on what principle? The keeping of the law would not exclude it, but faith does. For our argument is that a man is justified by faith quite apart from success in keeping the law. Do you suppose God is the God of the Jews alone? Is he not the God of Gentiles also? Certainly, of Gentiles also, if it be true that God is one. And he will therefore justify both the circumcised in virtue of their faith, and the uncircumcised through their faith. Does this mean that we are using faith to undermine law? By no means: we are placing law itself on a firmer footing. **Romans 3: 21-31 NEB~**

THE GOOD NEWS—THE GOSPEL

An angel of the Lord said to Philip, "Get ready and go south to the road that goes from Jerusalem to Gaza." (This road is not used nowadays.) So Philip got ready and went. Now an Ethiopian eunuch, who was an important official in charge of the treasury of the queen of Ethiopia, was on his way home. He had been to Jerusalem to worship God and was going back home in his carriage. As he rode along, he was reading from the book of the prophet Isaiah. The Holy Spirit said to Philip, "Go over to that carriage and stay close to it." Philip ran over and heard him reading from the book of the prophet Isaiah. He asked him, "Do you understand what you are reading?" The official replied, "How can I understand unless someone explains it to me?" And he invited Philip to climb up and sit in the carriage with him. The passage of scripture which he was reading was this: "He was like a sheep that is taken to be slaughtered, like a lamb that makes no sound when its wool is cut off. He did not say a word. He was humiliated, and justice was denied him. No one will be able to tell about his descendants, because his life on earth has come to an end."

The official asked Philip, "Tell me, of whom is the prophet saying this? Of himself or of someone else?" Then Philip began to speak; starting from this passage of scripture, he told him the Good News about Jesus. As they traveled down the road, they came to a place where there was some water, and the official said, "Here is some water. What is to keep me from being baptized?" The official ordered the carriage to stop, and both Philip and the official went down into the water, and Philip baptized him. When they came up out of the water, the Spirit of the Lord took Philip away. The official did not see him again, but continued on his way, full of joy. Philip found himself in Ashdod; he went on to Caesarea, and on the way he preached the Good News in every town.
Acts 8: 26-40 GNB

Brothers, descendants of Abraham's family, and those Gentiles among you who fear God, the message of this salvation has been sent to us. For the people who live in Jerusalem and their rulers did not recognize him, and they fulfilled the sayings of the prophets that are read every Sabbath by condemning him. Though they found no basis for a death sentence, they asked Pilate to have him executed. When they had accomplished everything that was written about him, they took him

down from the cross and placed him in a tomb. But God raised him from the dead, and for many days he appeared to those who had accompanied him from Galilee to Jerusalem. These are now his witnesses to the people. And we proclaim to you the good news about the promise to our ancestors, that this promise God has fulfilled to us, their children, by raising Jesus, as also it is written in the second psalm, 'You are my Son; today I have fathered you.'
Acts 13: 26-33 NET

The same thing happened in Iconium when Paul and Barnabas went into the Jewish synagogue and spoke in such a way that a large group of both Jews and Greeks believed. But the Jews who refused to believe stirred up the Gentiles and poisoned their minds against the brothers. So they stayed there for a considerable time, speaking out courageously for the Lord, who testified to the message of his grace, granting miraculous signs and wonders to be performed through their hands. But the population of the city was divided; some sided with the Jews, and some with the apostles. When both the Gentiles and the Jews (together with their rulers) made an attempt to mistreat them and stone them, Paul and Barnabas learned about it and fled to the Lycaonian cities of Lystra and Derbe and the surrounding region. There they continued to proclaim the good news.
Acts 14: 1-7 NET

From Paul, a slave of Christ Jesus, called to be an apostle,

set apart for the gospel of God. This gospel he promised beforehand through his prophets in the holy scriptures, concerning his Son who was a descendant of David with reference to the flesh, who was appointed the Son-of-God-in-power according to the Holy Spirit by the resurrection from the dead, Jesus Christ our Lord. Through him we have received grace and our apostleship to bring about the obedience of faith among all the Gentiles on behalf of his name. You also are among them, called to belong to Jesus Christ. To all those loved by God in Rome, called to be saints: Grace and peace to you from God our Father and the Lord Jesus Christ!
Romans 1: 1-7 NET

I do not want you to be unaware, brothers, that I planned many times to come to you (but have been prevented from doing so until now) in order that I might have a harvest among you, just as I have had among the other Gentiles. I am obligated both to Greeks and non-Greeks, both to the wise and the foolish. That is why I am so eager to preach the gospel also to you who are at Rome. I am not ashamed of the gospel, because it is the power of God for the salvation of everyone who believes: first for the Jew, then for the Gentile. For in the gospel a righteousness from God is revealed, a righteousness that is by faith from first to last, just as it is written: "The righteous will live by faith."
Romans 1: 13-17 NIV

Now I want to make clear for you, brothers and sisters,

the gospel that I preached to you, that you received and on which you stand, and by which you are being saved, if you hold firmly to the message I preached to you – unless you believed in vain. For I passed on to you as of first importance what I also received – that Christ died for our sins according to the scriptures, and that he was buried, and that he was raised on the third day according to the scriptures, and that he appeared to Cephas, then to the twelve. Then he appeared to more than five hundred of the brothers and sisters at one time, most of whom are still alive, though some have fallen asleep. Then he appeared to James, then to all the apostles. Last of all, as though to one born at the wrong time, he appeared to me also. For I am the least of the apostles, unworthy to be called an apostle, because I persecuted the church of God. But by the grace of God I am what I am, and his grace to me has not been in vain. In fact, I worked harder than all of them – yet not I, but the grace of God with me. Whether then it was I or they, this is the way we preach and this is the way you believed. **I Corinthians 15: 1-11 NET**

In former generations this was not disclosed to the human race; but now it has been revealed by inspiration to his dedicated apostles and prophets, that through the Gospel the Gentiles are joint heirs with the Jews, part of the same body, sharers together in the promise made in Christ Jesus. Such is the gospel of which I was made a minister, by God's gift, bestowed unmerited on me in the working of his power. To me, who am less than the least of all God's people, he has granted of his grace the privilege of proclaiming to the Gentiles the good news of the unfathomable riches of Christ, and of bringing to light how his hidden purpose was to be put into effect. It was hidden for long ages in God the creator of the universe, in order that now, through the church, the wisdom of God in all its varied forms might be made known to the rulers and authorities in the realms of heaven. This is in accord with his age-long purpose, which he achieved in Christ Jesus our Lord. In him we have access to God with freedom, in the confidence born of trust in him. **Ephesians 3: 5-12 NEB**

Choice

"Now therefore fear the Lord, and serve him in sincerity and in faithfulness; put away the gods which your fathers served beyond the River, and in Egypt, and serve the Lord. And if you be unwilling to serve the Lord, choose this day whom you will serve, whether the gods your fathers served in the region beyond the River, or the gods of the Amorites in whose land you dwell; but as for me and my house, we will serve the Lord."

Then the people answered, "Far be it from us that we should forsake the Lord, to serve other gods; for it is the Lord our God who brought us and our fathers up from the land of Egypt, out of the house of bondage, and who did those great signs in our sight, and preserved us in all the way that we went, and among all the peoples through whom we passed; and the Lord drove out before us all the peoples, the Amorites who lived in the land; therefore we also will serve the Lord, for he is our God."

But Joshua said to the people, "You cannot serve the Lord; for he is a holy God; he is a jealous God; he will

not forgive your transgressions or your sins. If you forsake the Lord and serve foreign gods, then he will turn and do you harm, and consume you, after having done you good." And the people said to Joshua, "Nay; but we will serve the Lord." Then Joshua said to the people, "You are witnesses against yourselves that you have chosen the Lord, to serve him." And they said, "We are witnesses." He said, "Then put away the foreign gods which are among you, and incline your heart to the Lord, the God of Israel." And the people said to Joshua, "The Lord our God we will serve, and his voice we will obey."
Joshua 24: 14-24 RSV

Do you think I have come to bring peace on earth? No, I tell you, but rather division! For from now on there will be five in one household divided, three against two and two against three. They will be divided, father against son and son against father, mother against daughter and daughter against mother, mother-in-law against her daughter-in-law and daughter-in-law against mother-in-law."

Jesus also said to the crowds, "When you see a cloud rising in the west, you say at once, 'A rainstorm is coming,' and it does. And when you see the south wind blowing, you say, 'There will be scorching heat,' and there is. You hypocrites! You know how to interpret the appearance of the earth and the sky, but how can you not know how to interpret the present time?

"And why don't you judge for yourselves what is right? As you are going with your accuser before the magistrate, make an effort to settle with him on the way, so that he will not drag you before the judge, and the judge hand you over to the officer, and the officer throw you into prison. I tell you, you will never get out of there until you have paid the very last cent!" **Luke 12: 51-59 NET**

Large crowds were traveling with Jesus, and turning to them he said: "If anyone comes to me and does not hate his father and mother, his wife and children, his brothers and sisters—yes, even his own life—he cannot be my disciple. And anyone who does not carry his cross and follow me cannot be my disciple."

"Suppose one of you wants to build a tower. Will he not first sit down and estimate the cost to see if he has enough money to complete it? For if he lays the foundation and is not able to finish it, everyone who sees it will ridicule him, saying, 'This fellow began to build and was not able to finish.'"

"Or suppose a king is about to go to war against another king. Will he not first sit down and consider whether he is able with ten thousand men to oppose the one coming against him with twenty thousand? If he is not able, he will send a delegation while the other is still a long way off and will ask for terms of peace. In the same way, any of you who does not give up everything he has cannot be my disciple. **Luke 14: 25-33 NIV+**

So sin must no longer reign in your mortal body, exacting obedience to the body's desires. You must no longer put its several parts at sin's disposal, as implements for doing wrong. No: put yourselves at the disposal of God, as dead men raised to life; yield your bodies to him as implements for doing right; for sin shall no longer be your master, because you are no longer under law, but under the grace of God.

What then? Are we to sin, because we are not under law but under grace? Of course not. You know well enough that if you put yourselves at the disposal of a master, to obey him, you are slaves of the master whom you obey; and this is true whether you serve sin, with death as its result; or obedience, with righteousness as its result. But God be thanked, you, who once were slaves of sin, have yielded whole-hearted obedience to the pattern of teaching to which you were made subject, and, emancipated from sin, have become slaves of righteousness (to use words that suit your human weakness)—I mean, as you once yielded your bodies to the service of impurity and lawlessness, making for moral anarchy, so now you must yield them to the service of righteousness, making for a holy life.

When you were slaves of sin, you were free from the control of righteousness; and what was the gain? Nothing but what now makes you ashamed, for the end of that is death. But now, freed from the commands of sin and bound to the service of God, your gains are such as make for holiness, and the end is eternal life. For sin pays a wage, and the wage is death, but God gives freely, and his gift is eternal life, in union with Christ Jesus our Lord. **Romans 6: 12-23 NEB**

For if I preach the gospel, I have no reason for boasting, because I am compelled to do this. Woe to me if I do not preach the gospel! For if I do this voluntarily, I have a reward. But if I do it unwillingly, I am entrusted with a responsibility. What then is my reward? That when I preach the gospel I may offer the gospel free of charge, and so not make full use of my rights in the gospel.

For since I am free from all I can make myself a slave to all, in order to gain even more people. To the Jews I became like a Jew to gain the Jews. To those under the law I became like one under the law (though I myself am not under the law) to gain those under the law. To those free from the law I became like one free from the law (though I am not free from God's law but under the law of Christ) to gain those free from the law. To the weak I became weak in order to gain the weak. I have become all things to all people, so that by all means I may save some. I do all these things because of the gospel, so that I can be a participant in it. **I Corinthians 9: 16-23 NET**

Humility

Thus Solomon finished the house of the Lord and the king's house; all that Solomon had planned to do in the house of the Lord and in his own house he successfully accomplished. Then the Lord appeared to Solomon in the night and said to him: "I have heard your prayer, and have chosen this place for myself as a house of sacrifice. When I shut up the heavens so that there is no rain, or command the locust to devour the land, or send pestilence among my people, if my people who are called by my name humble themselves, and pray and seek my face, and turn from their wicked ways, then I will hear from heaven, and will forgive their sin and heal their land."
II Chronicles 7: 11-14 RSV

And here is another parable that he told. It was aimed at those who were sure of their own goodness and looked down on everyone else. 'Two men went up to the temple to pray, one a Pharisee and the other a tax-gatherer. The Pharisee stood up and prayed thus: "I thank thee, O God, that I am not like the rest of men, greedy,

dishonest, adulterous; or, for that matter, like this tax-gatherer. I fast twice a week; I pay tithes on all that I get." But the other kept his distance and would not even raise his eyes to heaven, but beat upon his breast, saying, "O God, have mercy on me, sinner that I am." It was this man, I tell you, and not the other, who went home acquitted of his sins. For everyone who exalts himself will be humbled; and whoever humbles himself will be exalted.'
Luke 18: 9-14 NEB

Then when Jesus noticed how the guests chose the places of honor, he told them a parable. He said to them, "When you are invited by someone to a wedding feast, do not take the place of honor, because a person more distinguished than you may have been invited by your host. So the host who invited both of you will come and say to you, 'Give this man your place.' Then, ashamed, you will begin to move to the least important place. But when you are invited, go and take the least important place, so that when your host approaches he will say to you, 'Friend, move up here to a better place.' Then you will be honored in the presence of all who share the meal with you. For everyone who exalts himself will be humbled, but the one who humbles himself will be exalted."

He said also to the man who had invited him, "When you host a dinner or a banquet, don't invite your friends or your brothers or your relatives or rich neighbors so

you can be invited by them in return and get repaid. But when you host an elaborate meal, invite the poor, the crippled, the lame, and the blind. Then you will be blessed, because they cannot repay you, for you will be repaid at the resurrection of the righteous." When one of those at the meal with Jesus heard this, he said to him, "Blessed is everyone who will feast in the kingdom of God!"
Luke 14: 7-15 NET

Then little children were brought to Jesus for him to place his hands on them and pray for them. But the disciples rebuked those who brought them. Jesus said, "Let the little children come to me, and do not hinder them, for the kingdom of heaven belongs to such as these." When he had placed his hands on them, he went on from there. **Matthew 19: 13-15 NIV**

Jesus called them together and said, "You know that the rulers of the Gentiles lord it over them, and their high officials exercise authority over them. Not so with you. Instead, whoever wants to become great among you must be your servant, and whoever wants to be first must be your slave—just as the Son of Man did not come to be served, but to serve, and to give his life as a ransom for many." **Matthew 20: 25-28 NIV**

At that time the disciples came to Jesus, asking, "Who is the greatest in the Kingdom of heaven?" So Jesus called a child, had him stand in front of them, and said,

"I assure you that unless you change and become like children, you will never enter the Kingdom of heaven. The greatest in the Kingdom of heaven is the one who humbles himself and becomes like this child. And whoever welcomes in my name one such child as this, welcomes me.
Matthew 18: 1-8 GNB

If then our common life in Christ yields anything to stir the heart, any loving consolation, any sharing of the Spirit, any warmth of affection or compassion, fill up my cup of happiness by thinking and feeling alike, with the same love for one another, the same turn of mind, and a common care for unity. There must be no room for rivalry and personal vanity among you, but you must humbly reckon others better than yourselves. Look to each other's interest and not merely to your own.

Let your bearing towards one another arise out of your life in Christ Jesus. For the divine nature was his from the first; yet he did not think to snatch at equality with God, but made himself nothing, assuming the nature of a slave. Bearing the human likeness, revealed in human shape, he humbled himself, and in obedience accepted even death—death on a cross. Therefore God raised him to the heights and bestowed on him the name above all names, that at the name of Jesus every knee should bow—in heaven, on earth, and in the depths—and every tongue confess, 'Jesus Christ is Lord', to the glory of God the Father. **Philippians 2: 1-11 NEB+**

This doctrine of the cross is sheer folly to those on their way to ruin, but to us who are on the way to salvation it is the power of God. Scripture says, 'I will destroy the wisdom of the wise, and bring to nothing the cleverness of the clever.' Where is your wise man now, your man of learning, or your subtle debater—limited, all of them, to this passing age? God has made the wisdom of this world look foolish. As God in his wisdom ordained, the world failed to find him by its wisdom, and he chose to save those who have faith by the folly of the Gospel. Jews call for miracles, Greeks look for wisdom; but we proclaim Christ—yes, Christ nailed to the cross; and though this is a stumbling-block to Jews and folly to Greeks, yet to those who have heard his call, Jews and Greeks alike, he is the power of God and the wisdom of God.

Divine folly is wiser than the wisdom of man, and divine weakness stronger than man's strength. My brothers, think what sort of people you are, whom God has called. Few of you are men of wisdom, by any human standard; few are powerful or highly born. Yet, to shame the wise, God has chosen what the world counts folly, and to shame what is strong, God has chosen what the world counts weakness. He has chosen things low and contemptible, mere nothings, to overthrow the existing order. And so there is no place for human pride in the presence of God. You are in Christ Jesus by God's act, for God has made him our wisdom; he is our righteousness; in him we are consecrated and set free. And so (in the words of Scripture), 'If a man is proud, let him be proud of the Lord.'

As for me, brothers, when I came to you, I declared the attested truth of God without display of fine words or wisdom. I resolved that while I was with you I would think of nothing but Jesus Christ—Christ nailed to the cross. I came before you weak, as I was then, nervous and shaking with fear. The word I spoke, the gospel I proclaimed, did not sway you with subtle arguments; it carried conviction by spiritual power, so that your faith might be built not upon human wisdom but upon the power of God. **I Corinthians 1: 18- 2: 5 NEB**

For, I think, God has exhibited us apostles last of all, as men condemned to die, because we have become a spectacle to the world, both to angels and to people. We are fools for Christ, but you are wise in Christ! We are weak, but you are strong! You are distinguished, we are dishonored! To the present hour we are hungry and thirsty, poorly clothed, brutally treated, and without a roof over our heads. We do hard work, toiling with our own hands. When we are verbally abused, we respond with a blessing, when persecuted, we endure, when people lie about us, we answer in a friendly manner. We are the world's dirt and scum, even now.
I Corinthians 4: 9-13 NET

Scripture tells us that if a man needs to boast he should boast about what our Lord has done. Receiving approval from the Lord is what's important—not merely bragging about one-self. **II Corinthians 10: 17-18 HOV**

And so, to keep me from being unduly elated by the magnificence of such revelations, I was given a sharp pain in my body which came as Satan's messenger to bruise me; this was to save me from being unduly elated. Three times I begged the Lord to rid me of it, but his answer was: 'My grace is all you need; power comes to its full strength in weakness.' I shall therefore prefer to find my joy and pride in the very things that are my weakness; and then the power of Christ will come and rest upon me. Hence I am well content, for Christ's sake, with weakness, contempt, persecution, hardship, and frustration; for when I am weak, then I am strong. **II Corinthians 12: 7-10 NEB**

But how is it to your credit if you receive a beating for doing wrong and endure it? But if you suffer for doing good and you endure it, this is commendable before God. To this you were called, because Christ suffered for you, leaving you an example, that you should follow in his steps. "He committed no sin, and no deceit was found in his mouth." When they hurled their insults at him, he did not retaliate; when he suffered, he made no threats. Instead, he entrusted himself to him who judges justly. He himself bore our sins in his body on the tree, so that we might die to sins and live for righteousness; by his wounds you have been healed. For you were like sheep going astray, but now you have returned to the Shepherd and Overseer of your souls. **I Peter 2: 20-25 NIV+**

And all of you must put on the apron of humility, to serve one another; for the scripture says, "God resists the proud, but shows favor to the humble." Humble yourselves, then, under God's mighty hand, so that he will lift you up in his own good time. Leave all your worries with him, because he cares for you. **I Peter 5: 5-7 GNB**

COMMITMENT

After John was put in prison, Jesus went into Galilee, proclaiming the good news of God. "The time has come," he said. "The kingdom of God is near. Repent and believe the good news!" As Jesus walked beside the Sea of Galilee, he saw Simon and his brother Andrew casting a net into the lake, for they were fishermen. "Come, follow me," Jesus said, "and I will make you fishers of men." At once they left their nets and followed him. When he had gone a little farther, he saw James son of Zebedee and his brother John in a boat, preparing their nets. Without delay he called them, and they left their father Zebedee in the boat with the hired men and followed him. **Mark 1: 14-20 NIV**

As Jesus sat near the temple treasury, he watched the people as they dropped in their money. Many rich men dropped in a lot of money; then a poor widow came along and dropped in two little copper coins, worth about a penny. He called his disciples together and said to them, "I tell you that this poor widow put more in the offering box than all the others. For the

others put in what they had to spare of their riches; but she, poor as she is, put in all she had—she gave all she had to live on."
Mark 12: 41-44 GNB

Entering Jericho he made is way through the city. There was a man there named Zacchaeus; he was superintendent of taxes and very rich. He was eager to see what Jesus looked like; but, being a little man, he could not see him for the crowd. So he ran on ahead and climbed a sycamore tree in order to see him, for he was to pass that way. When Jesus came to the place, he looked up and said 'Zacchaeus, be quick and come down; I must come and stay with you today.' He climbed down as fast as he could and welcomed him gladly. At this there was a general murmur of disapproval. 'He has gone in', they said, 'to be the guest of a sinner.' But Zacchaeus stood there and said to the Lord, 'Here and now, sir, I give half my possessions to charity; and if I have cheated anyone, I am ready to repay him four times over.' Jesus said to him, 'Salvation has come to this house today!—for this man too is a son of Abraham, and the Son of Man has come to seek and save what is lost.' **Luke 19: 1-10 NEB**

Now someone came up to him and said, "Teacher, what good thing must I do to gain eternal life?" He said to him, "Why do you ask me about what is good? There is only one who is good. But if you want to enter into life, keep the commandments." "Which ones?" he asked.

Jesus replied, "Do not murder, do not commit adultery, do not steal, do not give false testimony, honor your father and mother, and love your neighbor as yourself." The young man said to him, "I have wholeheartedly obeyed all these laws. What do I still lack?" Jesus said to him, "If you wish to be perfect, go sell your possessions and give the money to the poor, and you will have treasure in heaven. Then come, follow me."

But when the young man heard this he went away sorrowful, for he was very rich. Then Jesus said to his disciples, "I tell you the truth, it will be hard for a rich person to enter the kingdom of heaven! Again I say, it is easier for a camel to go through the eye of a needle than for a rich person to enter into the kingdom of God." The disciples were greatly astonished when they heard this and said, "Then who can be saved?" Jesus looked at them and replied, "This is impossible for mere humans, but for God all things are possible." **Matthew 19:16-26 NET~**

To the Jews who had believed him, Jesus said, "If you hold to my teaching, you are really my disciples. Then you will know the truth, and the truth will set you free." **John 8: 31-32 NIV**

Then he said to them, "Suppose one of you has a friend, and you go to him at midnight and say to him, 'Friend, lend me three loaves of bread, because a friend of mine has stopped here while on a journey, and I have nothing to set before him.' Then he will reply from inside, 'Do not bother me. The door is already shut, and my children and I are in bed. I cannot get up and give you anything.' I tell you, even though the man inside will not get up and give him anything because he is his friend, yet because of the first man's sheer persistence he will get up and give him whatever he needs.

"So I tell you: Ask, and it will be given to you; seek, and you will find; knock, and the door will be opened for you. For everyone who asks receives, and the one who seeks finds, and to the one who knocks, the door will be opened. What father among you, if your son asks for a fish, will give him a snake instead of a fish? Or if he asks for an egg, will give him a scorpion? If you then, although you are evil, know how to give good gifts to your children, how much more will the heavenly Father give the Holy Spirit to those who ask him!" **Luke 11: 5-13 NET**

So they brought them and stood them before the Council; and the High Priest began his examination. 'We expressly ordered you', he said, 'to desist from teaching in that name; and what has happened? You have filled Jerusalem with your teaching, and you are trying to make us responsible for that man's death.' Peter replied for himself and the apostles: 'We must obey God rather than men. The God of our fathers raised up Jesus whom you had done to death by hanging him on a gibbet. He is whom God has exalted with his own right hand as leader and savior, to grant Israel repentance and forgiveness of sins. And we are witnesses to all this, and so is the Holy Spirit given by God to those who are obedient to him.' **Acts 5: 27-32 NEB**

As the members of the Council listened to Stephen, they became furious and ground their teeth at him in anger. But Stephen, full of the Holy Spirit, looked up to heaven and saw God's glory and Jesus standing at the right side of God. "Look!" he said. "I see heaven opened and the Son of Man standing at the right side of God!" With a loud cry the Council members covered their ears with their hands. Then they all rushed at him at once, threw him out of the city, and stoned him. The witnesses left their cloaks in the care of a young man named Saul. They kept on stoning Stephen as he called out to the Lord, "Lord Jesus, receive my spirit!" He knelt down and cried out in a loud voice, "Lord! Do not remember this sin against them!" He said this and died.
Acts 7: 54-60 GNB

About that time King Herod laid hands on some from the church to harm them. He had James, the brother of John, executed with a sword. When he saw that this pleased the Jews, he proceeded to arrest Peter too. (This took place during the feast of Unleavened Bread.) When he had seized him, he put him in prison, handing him over to four squads of soldiers to guard him. Herod planned to bring him out for public trial after the Passover. So Peter was kept in prison, but those in the church were earnestly praying to God for him. On that very night before Herod was going to bring him out for trial, Peter was sleeping between two soldiers, bound with two chains, while guards in front of the door were keeping watch over the prison. Suddenly an angel of the Lord appeared, and a light shone in the prison cell. He struck Peter on the side and woke him up, saying, "Get up quickly!" And the chains fell off Peter's wrists. The angel said to him, "Fasten your belt and put on your sandals." Peter did so. Then the angel said to him, "Put on your cloak and follow me." Peter went out and followed him; he did not realize that what was happening through the angel was real, but thought he was seeing a vision. After they had passed the first and second guards, they came to the iron gate leading into the city. It opened for them by itself, and they went outside and walked down one narrow street, when at once the angel left him. When Peter came to himself, he said, "Now I know for certain that the Lord has sent his angel and rescued me from the hand of Herod and from everything the Jewish people were expecting to happen."

When Peter realized this, he went to the house of Mary, the mother of John Mark, where many people had gathered together and were praying. When he knocked at the door of the outer gate, a slave girl named Rhoda answered. When she recognized Peter's voice, she was so overjoyed she did not open the gate, but ran back in and told them that Peter was standing at the gate. But they said to her, "You've lost your mind!" But she kept insisting that it was Peter, and they kept saying, "It is his angel!" Now Peter continued knocking, and when they opened the door and saw him, they were greatly astonished. He motioned to them with his hand to be quiet and then related how the Lord had brought him out of the prison. He said, "Tell James and the brothers these things," and then he left and went to another place.

At daybreak there was great consternation among the soldiers over what had become of Peter. When Herod had searched for him and did not find him, he questioned the guards and commanded that they be led away to execution. Then Herod went down from Judea to Caesarea and stayed there. **Acts 12: 1-19 NET**

Then some Jews came from Antioch and Iconium and won the crowd over. They stoned Paul and dragged him outside the city, thinking he was dead. But after the disciples had gathered around him, he got up and went back into the city. The next day he and Barnabas left for Derbe. They preached the good news in that city and won a large number of disciples. Then they returned to Lystra, Iconium and Antioch, strengthening the disciples and encouraging them to remain true to the faith. "We must go through many hardships to enter the kingdom of God," they said. Paul and Barnabas appointed elders for them in each church and, with prayer and fasting, committed them to the Lord, in whom they had put their trust.
Acts 14: 19-23 NIV

Do you not know that in a race all the runners run, but only one gets the prize? Run in such a way as to get the prize. Everyone who competes in the games goes into strict training. They do it to get a crown that will not last; but we do it to get a crown that will last forever. Therefore I do not run like a man running aimlessly; I do not fight like a man beating the air. No, I beat my body and make it my slave so that after I have preached to others, I myself will not be disqualified for the prize. **I Corinthians 9: 24-27 NIV**

If you feel sure that you are standing firm, beware! You may fall. So far you have faced no trial beyond what man can bear. God keeps faith, and he will not allow you to be tested above your powers, but when the test comes he will at the same time provide a way out, by enabling you to sustain it. **I Corinthians 10: 12-13 NEB**

We are no better than pots of earthenware to contain this treasure, and this proves that such transcendent power does not come from us, but is God's alone. Hard-pressed on every side, we are never hemmed in; bewildered, we are never at our wits' end; hunted, we are never abandoned to our fate; struck down, we are not left to die. Wherever we go we carry death with us in our body, the death that Jesus died, that in his body also life may reveal itself, the life that Jesus lives. For continually, while still alive, we are being surrendered into the hands of death, for Jesus' sake, so that the life of Jesus also may be revealed in this mortal body of ours. Thus death is at work in us, and life in you. **II Corinthians 4: 7-13 NEB**

In order that our service may not be brought into discredit, we avoid giving offence in anything. As God's servants, we try to recommend ourselves in all circumstances by our steadfast endurance: in hardships and dire straits; flogged, imprisoned, mobbed; overworked, sleepless, starving. We recommend ourselves by the innocence of our behavior, our grasp of truth, our patience and kindliness; by gifts of the Holy Spirit, by sincere love, by declaring the truth, by the power of God. We wield the weapons of righteousness in right hand and left. Honor and dishonor, praise and blame, are alike our lot: we are the impostors who speak the truth, the unknown men whom all men know; dying we still live on; disciplined by suffering, we are not done to death; in our sorrows we have always cause for joy; poor ourselves, we bring wealth to many; penniless, we own the world. **II Corinthians 6: 3-10 NEB**

My brothers, consider yourselves fortunate when all kinds of trials come your way, for you know that when your faith succeeds in facing such trials, the result is the ability to endure. Make sure that your endurance caries you all the way without failing, so that you may be perfect and complete, lacking nothing. But if any of you lacks wisdom, he should pray to God, who will give it to him; because God gives generously and graciously to all. But when you pray, you must believe and not doubt at all. Whoever doubts is like a wave in the sea that is driven and blown about by the wind. A person like that, unable to make up his mind and undecided in all he does, must not think that he will receive anything from the Lord. **James 1: 2-8 GNB**

Now we make known to you, brothers and sisters, the grace of God given to the churches of Macedonia, that during a severe ordeal of suffering, their abundant joy and their extreme poverty have overflowed in the wealth of their generosity. For I testify, they gave according to their means and beyond their means. They did so voluntarily, begging us with great earnestness for the blessing and fellowship of helping the saints. And they did this not just as we had hoped, but they gave themselves first to the Lord and to us by the will of God.

Thus we urged Titus that, just as he had previously begun this work, so also he should complete this act of kindness for you. But as you excel in everything – in faith, in speech, in knowledge, and in all eagerness and in the love from us that is in you – make sure that you excel in this act of kindness too. I am not saying this as a command, but I am testing the genuineness of your love by comparison with the eagerness of others. For you know the grace of our Lord Jesus Christ, that although he was rich, he became poor for your sakes, so that you by his poverty could become rich.

So here is my opinion on this matter: It is to your advantage, since you made a good start last year both in your giving and your desire to give, to finish what you started, so that just as you wanted to do it eagerly, you can also complete it according to your means. For if the eagerness is present, the gift itself is acceptable according to whatever one has, not according to what he does not have. For I do not say this so there would be relief for others and suffering for you, but as a matter of equality. At the present time, your abundance will meet their need, so that one day their abundance may also meet your need, and thus there may be equality, as it is written: "The one who gathered much did not have too much, and the one who gathered little did not have too little."

II Corinthians 8: 1-15 NET

I repeat: let no one take me for a fool; but if you must, then give me the privilege of a fool, and let me have my little boast like others. I am not speaking here as a Christian, but like a fool, if it comes to bragging. So many people brag of their earthly distinctions that I shall do so too. How gladly you bear with fools, being yourselves so wise! If a man tyrannizes over you, exploits you, gets you in his clutches, puts on airs, and hits you in the face, you put up with it. And we, you say, have been weak! I admit the reproach.

But if there is to be bravado (and here I speak as a fool), I can indulge in it too. Are they Hebrews? So am I.

Israelites? So am I. Abraham's descendants? So am I. Are they servants of Christ? I am mad to speak like this, but I can outdo them. More overworked than they, scourged more severely, more often imprisoned, many a times face to face with death. Five times the Jews have given me the thirty-nine strokes; three times I have been beaten with rods; once I was stoned; three times I have been shipwrecked, and for twenty-four hours I was adrift on the open sea. I have been constantly on the road; I have met dangers from rivers, dangers from robbers, dangers from my fellow-countrymen, dangers from foreigners, dangers in towns, dangers in the country, dangers at sea, dangers from false friends. I have toiled and drudged, I have often gone without sleep; hungry and thirsty, I have often gone fasting; and I have suffered from cold and exposure.

Apart from these external things, there is the responsibility that weighs on me every day, my anxious concern for all our congregations. If anyone is weak, do I not share his weakness? If anyone is made to stumble, does my heart not blaze with indignation? If boasting there must be, I will boast of the things that show up my weakness. The God and Father of the Lord Jesus (blessed be his name for ever!) knows that what I say is true. When I was in Damascus, the commissioner of King Aretas kept the city under observation so as to have me arrested; and I was let down in a basket, through a window in the wall, and so escaped his clutches.
II Corinthians 11: 16-33 NEB

Finally, be strengthened in the Lord and in the strength of his power. Clothe yourselves with the full armor of God so that you may be able to stand against the schemes of the devil. For our struggle is not against flesh and blood, but against the rulers, against the powers, against the world rulers of this darkness, against the spiritual forces of evil in the heavens. For this reason, take up the full armor of God so that you may be able to stand your ground on the evil day, and having done everything, to stand. Stand firm therefore, by fastening the belt of truth around your waist, by putting on the breastplate of righteousness, by fitting your feet with the preparation that comes from the good news of peace, and in all of this, by taking up the shield of faith with which you can extinguish all the flaming arrows of the evil one. And take the helmet of salvation and the sword of the Spirit, which is the word of God. With every prayer and petition, pray at all times in the Spirit, and to this end be alert, with all perseverance and requests for all the saints. Pray for me also, that I may be given the message when I begin to speak – that I may confidently make known the mystery of the gospel, for which I am an ambassador in chains. Pray that I may be able to speak boldly as I ought to speak. **Ephesians 6: 10-20 NET~**

MISSION

Then God said, "Let us make man in our image, after our likeness; and let them have dominion over the fish of the sea, and over the birds of the air, and over the cattle, and over all the earth, and over every creeping thing that creeps upon the earth." So God created man in his own image, in the image of God he created him; male and female he created them. And God blessed them, and God said to them, "Be fruitful and multiply, and fill the earth and subdue it; and have dominion over the fish of the sea and over the birds of the air and over every living thing that moves upon the earth." And God said, "Behold, I have given you every plant yielding seed which is upon the face of all the earth, and every tree with seed in its fruit; you shall have them for food. And to every beast of the earth, and to every bird of the air, and to everything that creeps on the earth, everything that has the breath of life, I have given every green plant for food." And it was so. And God saw everything that he had made, and behold, it was very good. **Genesis 1: 26-31 RSV**

Now the Lord said to Abram, "Go from your country and your kindred and your father's house to the land that I will show you. And I will make of you a great nation, and I will bless you, and make your name great, so that you will be a blessing. I will bless those who bless you, and him who curses you I will curse; and by you all the families of the earth will bless themselves." **Genesis 12: 1-3 RSV**

Blessed are all who fear the LORD, who walk in his ways. You will eat the fruit of your labor; blessings and prosperity will be yours. Your wife will be like a fruitful vine within your house; your sons will be like olive shoots around your table. Thus is the man blessed who fears the LORD. May the LORD bless you from Zion all the days of your life; may you see the prosperity of Jerusalem, and may you live to see your children's children. Peace be upon Israel. **Psalms 128: 1-6 NIV**

A shoot will come up from the stump of Jesse; from his roots a Branch will bear fruit. The Spirit of the LORD will rest on him—the Spirit of wisdom and of understanding, the Spirit of counsel and of power, the Spirit of knowledge and of the fear of the LORD—and he will delight in the fear of the LORD. He will not judge by what he sees with his eyes, or decide by what he hears with his ears; but with righteousness he will judge the needy, with justice he will give decisions for the poor of the earth. He will strike the earth with the rod of his mouth; with the breath of his lips he will slay the wicked. Righteousness will be his belt and faithfulness the sash around his waist. The wolf will live with the lamb, the leopard will lie down with the goat, the calf and the lion and the yearling together; and a little child will lead them. The cow will feed with the bear, their young will lie down together, and the lion will eat straw like the ox. The infant will play near the hole of the cobra, and the young child put his hand into the viper's nest. They will neither harm nor destroy on all my holy mountain, for the earth will be full of the knowledge of the LORD as the waters cover the sea. **Isaiah 11: 1-9 NIV**

And Jesus went about all the cities and villages, teaching in their synagogues and preaching the gospel of the kingdom, and healing every disease and every infirmity. When he saw the crowds, he had compassion for them, because they were harassed and helpless, like sheep without a shepherd. Then he said to his disciples, "The harvest is plentiful, but the laborers are few; pray therefore the Lord of the harvest to send out laborers into his harvest." **Matthew 9: 35-38 RSV**

Jesus continued, "Does anyone ever bring in a lamp and put it under a bowl or under the bed? Doesn't he put it on the lampstand? Whatever is hidden away will be brought out into the open, and whatever is covered up will be uncovered. Listen, then, if you have ears!" **Mark 4: 21-23 GNB**

Among those who went up to worship at the festival were some Greeks. They came to Philip, who was from Bethsaida in Galilee, and said to him, 'Sir, we should like to see Jesus.' So Philip went and told Andrew, and the two of them went to tell Jesus. Then Jesus replied: 'The hour has come for the Son of Man to be glorified. In truth, in very truth I tell you, a grain of wheat remains a solitary grain unless it falls into the ground and dies; but if it dies, it bears a rich harvest. The man who loves himself is lost, but he who hates himself in this world will be kept safe for eternal life. If anyone serves me, he must follow me; where I am, my servant will be. Whoever serves me will be honored by my Father.
John 12: 20-26 NEB

"I am the real vine, and my Father is the gardener. He breaks off every branch in me that does not bear fruit, and he prunes every branch that does bear fruit, so that it will be clean and bear more fruit. You have been made clean already by the teaching I have given you. Remain united to me, and I will remain united to you. A branch cannot bear fruit by itself; it can do so only if it remains in the vine. In the same way you cannot bear fruit unless you remain in me.

"I am the vine, and you are the branches. Whoever remains in me, and I in him, will bear much fruit; for you can do nothing without me. Whoever does not remain in me is thrown out like a branch and dries up; such branches are gathered up and thrown into the fire, where they are burned. If you remain in me and my words remain in you, then you will ask for anything you wish, and you shall have it. My Father's glory is shown by your bearing much fruit; and in this way you become my disciples. I love you just as the Father loves me; remain in my love. If you obey my commands, you will remain in my love, just as I have obeyed my Father's commands and remain in his love.

I have told you this so that my joy may be in you and that your joy may be complete. My commandment is this: love one another, just as I love you. The greatest love a person can have for his friends is to give his life for them. And you are my friends if you do what I command you. I do not call you servants any longer, because a servant does not know what his master is doing. Instead, I call you friends, because I have told you everything I heard from my Father. You did not choose me; I chose you and appointed you to go and bear much fruit, the kind of fruit that endures. And so the Father will give you whatever you ask of him in my name. This, then, is what I command you: love one another. **John 15: 1-17 GNB+**

When Jesus had finished saying these things, he looked upward to heaven and said, "Father, the time has come. Glorify your Son, so that your Son may glorify you – just as you have given him authority over all humanity, so that he may give eternal life to everyone you have given him. Now this is eternal life – that they know you, the only true God, and Jesus Christ, whom you sent. I glorified you on earth by completing the work you gave me to do. And now, Father, glorify me at your side with the glory I had with you before the world was created.

"I have revealed your name to the men you gave me out of the world. They belonged to you, and you gave them to me, and they have obeyed your word. Now they understand that everything you have given me comes from you, because I have given them the words you have given me. They accepted them and really understand that I came from you, and they believed that you sent me. I am praying on behalf of them. I am not praying on behalf of the world, but on behalf of those you have given me, because they belong to you. Everything I have belongs to you, and everything you have belongs to me, and I have been glorified by them. I am no longer in the world, but they are in the world, and I am coming to you. Holy Father, keep them safe in your name that you have given me, so that they may be one just as we are one. When I was with them I kept them safe and watched over them in your name that you have given me. Not one of them was lost except the one destined for destruction, so that the scripture could be fulfilled. But now I am coming to you, and I am saying these things in the world, so they may experience my joy completed in themselves. I have given them your word, and the world has hated them, because they do not belong to the world, just as I do not belong to the world. I am not asking you to take them out of the world, but that you keep them safe from the evil one. They do not belong to the world just as I do not belong to the world. Set them apart in the truth; your word is truth. Just as you sent me into the world, so I sent them into the world. And I set myself apart on their behalf, so that they too may be truly set apart.

"I am not praying only on their behalf, but also on behalf of those who believe in me through their testimony, that they will all be one, just as you, Father, are in me and I am in you. I pray that they will be in us, so that the world will believe that you sent me. The glory you gave to me I have given to them, that they may be one just as we are one – I in them and you in me – that they may be completely one, so that the world will know that you sent me, and you have loved them just as you have loved me.

"Father, I want those you have given me to be with me where I am, so that they can see my glory that you gave me because you loved me before the creation of the world. Righteous Father, even if the world does not know you, I know you, and these men know that you sent me. I made known your name to them, and I will continue to make it known, so that the love you have loved me with may be in them, and I may be in them."
John 17:1-26 NET

And Jesus came and said to them, "All authority in heaven and on earth has been given to me. Go therefore

and make disciples of all nations, baptizing them in the name of the Father and of the Son and of the Holy Spirit, teaching them to observe all that I have commanded you; and lo, I am with you always, to the close of the age."
Matthew 28: 18-20 RSV*

My friends, I have no doubt in my own mind that you yourselves are quite full of goodness and equipped with knowledge of every kind, well able to give advice to one another; nevertheless I have written to refresh your memory, and written somewhat boldly at times, in virtue of the gift I have from God. His grace has made me a minister of Christ Jesus to the Gentiles; my priestly service is the preaching of the gospel of God, and it falls to me to offer the Gentiles to him as an acceptable sacrifice, consecrated by the Holy Spirit.

Thus in the fellowship of Christ Jesus I have ground for pride in the service of God. I will venture to speak of those things alone in which I have been Christ's instrument to bring the Gentiles into his allegiance, by word and deed, by the force of miraculous signs and by the power of the Holy Spirit. As a result I have completed the preaching of the gospel of Christ from Jerusalem as far round as Illyricum. It is my ambition to bring the gospel to places where the very name of Christ has not been heard, for I do not want to build on another man's foundation; but, as Scripture says, 'They who had no news of him shall see, and they who never heard of him shall understand.' **Romans 15: 14-21 NEB**

We are coworkers belonging to God. You are God's field, God's building. According to the grace of God given to me, like a skilled master-builder I laid a foundation, but someone else builds on it. And each one must be careful how he builds. For no one can lay any foundation other than what is being laid, which is Jesus Christ. If anyone builds on the foundation with gold, silver, precious stones, wood, hay, or straw, each builder's work will be plainly seen, for the Day will make it clear, because it will be revealed by fire. And the fire will test what kind of work each has done. If what someone has built survives, he will receive a reward. If someone's work is burned up, he will suffer loss. He himself will be saved, but only as through fire. Do you not know that you are God's temple and that God's Spirit lives in you? If someone destroys God's temple, God will destroy him. For God's temple is holy, which is what you are. **I Corinthians 3: 9-16 NET**

In the days of his flesh, Jesus offered up prayers and supplications, with loud cries and tears, to him who was able to save him from death, and he was heard for his godly fear. Although he was a Son, he learned obedience through what he suffered; and being made perfect he became the source of eternal salvation to all who obey him, being designated by God a high priest after the order of Melchizedek. **Hebrews 5: 7-10 RSV**

Seeing then that we have been entrusted with this commission, which we owe entirely to God's mercy, we never lose heart. We have renounced the deeds that men hide for very shame; we neither practice cunning nor distort the word of God; only by declaring the truth openly do we recommend ourselves, and then it is to the common conscience of our fellow-men and in the sight of God. And if indeed our gospel be found veiled, the only people who find it so are those on the way to perdition. Their unbelieving minds are so blinded by the god of this passing age, that the gospel of the glory of Christ, who is the very image of God, cannot dawn upon them and bring them light. It is not ourselves that we proclaim; we proclaim Christ Jesus as Lord, and ourselves as your servants, for Jesus' sake. For the same God who said, 'Out of darkness let light shine', has caused his light to shine within us, to give the light of revelation—the revelation of the glory of God in the face of Jesus Christ. **II Corinthians 4: 1-6 NEB**

Everyone must submit himself to the governing authorities, for there is no authority except that which God has established. The authorities that exist have been established by God. Consequently, he who rebels against the authority is rebelling against what God has instituted, and those who do so will bring judgment on themselves. For rulers hold no terror for those who do right, but for those who do wrong. Do you want to be free from fear of the one in authority? Then do what is right and he will commend you. For he is God's servant to do you good. But if you do wrong, be afraid, for he does not bear the sword for nothing. He is God's servant, an agent of wrath to bring punishment on the wrongdoer. Therefore, it is necessary to submit to the authorities, not only because of possible punishment but also because of conscience. This is also why you pay taxes, for the authorities are God's servants, who give their full time to governing. Give everyone what you owe him: If you owe taxes, pay taxes; if revenue, then revenue; if respect, then respect; if honor, then honor. **Romans 13: 1-7 NIV**

I want you to know, my brothers, that the things that have happened to me have really helped the progress of the gospel. As a result, the whole palace guard and all the others here know that I am in prison because I am a servant of Christ. And my being in prison has given most of the brothers more confidence in the Lord, so that they grow bolder all the time to preach the message fearlessly.

Of course some of them preach Christ because they are jealous and quarrelsome, but others from genuine good will. These do so from love, because they know that God has given me the work of defending the gospel. The others do not proclaim Christ sincerely, but from a spirit of selfish ambition; they think that they will make more trouble for me while I am in prison.

It does not matter! I am happy about it—just so Christ

is preached in every way possible, whether from wrong or right motives. And I will continue to be happy, because I know that by means of your prayers and the help which comes from the Spirit of Jesus Christ I shall be set free. My deep desire and hope is that I shall never fail in my duty, but that at all times, and especially right now, I shall be full of courage, so that with my whole being I shall bring honor to Christ, whether I live or die. For what is life? To me, it is Christ. Death, then, will bring more. But if by continuing to live I can do more worthwhile work, then I am not sure which I should choose. I am pulled in two directions. I want very much to leave this life and be with Christ, which is a far better thing; but for your sake it is much more important that I remain alive. I am sure of this, and so I know that I will stay. I will stay on with you all, to add to your progress and joy in the faith, so that when I am with you again, you will have even more reason to be proud of me in your life in union with Christ Jesus.

Now, the important thing is that your way of life should be as the gospel of Christ requires, so that, whether or not I am able to go and see you, I will hear that you are standing firm with one common purpose and that with only one desire you are fighting together for the faith of the gospel. Don't be afraid of your enemies; always be courageous, and this will prove to them that they will lose and that you will win because it is God who gives you the victory. For you have been given the privilege of serving Christ, not only by believing in him, but also by suffering for him. Now you can take part with me in the battle. It is the same battle you saw me fighting in the past, and as you hear, the one I am fighting still. **Philippians 1: 12-30 GNB**

Therefore, my beloved, as you have always obeyed, so now, not only as in my presence but much more in my absence, work out your own salvation with fear and trembling; for God is at work in you, both to will and to work for his good pleasure. Do all things without grumbling or questioning, that you may be blameless and innocent, children of God without blemish in the midst of a crooked and perverse generation, among whom you shine as lights in the world, holding fast the word of life, so that in the day of Christ I may be proud that I did not run in vain or labor in vain. Even if I am to be poured as a libation upon the sacrificial offering of your faith, I am glad and rejoice with you all. Likewise you also should be glad and rejoice with me. **Philippians 2: 12-18 RSV**

I do not claim that I have already succeeded or have already become perfect. I keep striving to win the prize for which Christ Jesus has already won me to himself. Of course, my brothers, I really do not think that I have already won it; the one thing I do, however, is to forget what is behind me and do my best to reach what is ahead. So I run straight toward the goal in order to win the prize, which is God's call through Christ Jesus to the life above. **Philippians 3: 12-14 GNB**

He (Paul) did, however, send from Miletus to Ephesus and summon the elders of the congregation; and when they joined him, he spoke as follows: 'You know how, from the day that I first set foot in the province of Asia, for the whole time that I was with you, I served the Lord in all humility amid the sorrows and trials that came upon me through the machinations of the Jews. You know that I kept back nothing that was for your good: I delivered the message to you; I taught you, in public and in your homes; with Jews and pagans alike I insisted on repentance before God and trust in our Lord Jesus. And now, as you see, I am on my way to Jerusalem, under the constraint of the Spirit. Of what will befall me there I know nothing, except that in city after city the Holy Spirit assures me that imprisonment and hardships await me. For myself, I set not store by life; I only want to finish the race, and complete the task which the Lord Jesus assigned to me, of bearing my testimony to the gospel of God's grace.

'One word more: I have gone about among you proclaiming the Kingdom, but now I know that none of you will see my face again. That being so, I here and now declare that no man's fate can be laid at my door; for I have kept back nothing; I have disclosed to you the whole purpose of God. Keep watch over yourselves and over all the flock of which the Holy Spirit has given you charge, as shepherds of the church of the Lord, which he won for himself by his own blood. I know that when I am gone, savage wolves will come in among you and will not spare the flock. Even from your own body there will be men coming forward who will distort the truth to induce the disciples to break away and follow them. So be on the alert; remember how for three years, night and day, I never ceased to counsel each of you, and how I wept over you.

'And now I commend you to God and to his gracious word, which has power to build you up and give you your heritage among all who are dedicated to him. I have not wanted anyone's money or clothes for myself; you all know that these hands of mine earned enough for the needs of me and my companions. I showed you that it is our duty to help the weak in this way, by hard work, and that we should keep in mind the words of the Lord Jesus, who himself said, "Happiness lies more in giving than in receiving."' As he finished speaking, he knelt down with them all and prayed. Then there were loud cries of sorrow from them all, as they folded Paul in their arms and kissed him. What distressed them most was his saying that they would never see his face again. So they escorted him to his ship. **Acts 20: 17-38 NEB**

God has appointed me as an apostle and teacher to proclaim the Good News, and it is for this reason that I suffer these things. But I am still full of confidence, because I know whom I have trusted, and I am sure that he is able to keep safe until that Day what he has entrusted to me. Hold firmly to the true words that

I taught you, as the example for you to follow, and remain in the faith and love that are ours in union with Christ Jesus. Through the power of the Holy Spirit, who lives in us, keep the good things that have been entrusted to you.
II Timothy 1: 11-14 GNB

Come to the Lord, the living stone rejected by man as worthless but chosen by God as valuable. Come as living stones, and let yourselves be used in building the spiritual temple, where you will serve as holy priests to offer spiritual and acceptable sacrifices to God through Jesus Christ. For the scripture says, "I chose a valuable stone, which I am placing as the cornerstone in Zion; and whoever believes in him will never be disappointed." This stone is of great value for you that believe; but for those who do not believe: "The stone which the builders rejected as worthless turned out to be the most important of all." And another scripture says, "This is the stone that will make people stumble, the rock that will make them fall." They stumbled because they did not believe in the word; such was God's will for them.

But you are the chosen race, the king's priests, the holy nation, God's own people, chosen to proclaim the wonderful acts of God, who called you out of darkness into his own marvelous light. At one time you were not God's people, but now you are his people; at one time you did not know God's mercy, but now you have received his mercy. **I Peter 2: 4-10 GNB**

LIFESTYLE

"When you reap the harvest of your land, do not reap to the very edges of your field or gather the gleanings of your harvest. Do not go over your vineyard a second time or pick up the grapes that have fallen. Leave them for the poor and the alien." I am the LORD your God.
Leviticus 19: 9-10 NIV

Praise the LORD. Blessed is the man who fears the LORD, who finds great delight in his commands. His children will be mighty in the land; the generation of the upright will be blessed. Wealth and riches are in his house, and his righteousness endures forever. Even in darkness light dawns for the upright, for the gracious and compassionate and righteous man. Good will come to him who is generous and lends freely, who conducts his affairs with justice. Surely he will never be shaken; a righteous man will be remembered forever.
Psalms 112: 1-6 NIV

"Not everyone who says to me, 'Lord, Lord,' will enter

the kingdom of heaven, but only he who does the will of my Father who is in heaven." **Matthew 7: 21 NIV**

"The kingdom of heaven is like treasure hidden in a field, which a man found and covered up; then in his joy he goes and sells all that he has and buys that field. Again, the kingdom of heaven is like a merchant in search of fine pearls, who, on finding one pearl of great value, went and sold all that he had and bought it. Again, the kingdom of heaven is like a net which was thrown into the sea and gathered fish of every kind; when it was full, men drew it ashore and sat down and sorted the good into vessels but threw away the bad. So it will be at the close of the age. The angels will come out and separate the evil from the righteous, and throw them into the furnace of fire; there men will weep and gnash their teeth."
Matthew 13: 44-50 RSV

At that time the Kingdom of heaven will be like this. Once there was a man who was about to leave home on a trip; he called his servants and put them in charge of his property. He gave to each one according to his ability: to one he gave five thousand silver coins, to another he gave two thousand, and to another he gave one thousand. Then he left on his trip. The servant who had received five thousand coins went at once and invested his money and earned another five thousand. In the same way the servant who had received two thousand coins earned another two thousand. But the servant who had received one thousand coins went off, dug a hole in the ground, and hid is master's money.

After a long time the master of those servants came back and settled accounts with them. The servant who had received five thousand coins came in and handed over the other five thousand. 'You gave me five thousand coins, sir,' he said. 'Look! Here are another five thousand that I have earned.' 'Well done, you good and faithful servant!' said his master. 'You have been faithful in managing small amounts, so I will put you in charge of large amounts. Come on in and share my happiness!' Then the servant who had been given two thousand coins came in and said, 'You gave me two thousand coins, sir. Look! Here are another two thousand that I have earned.' 'Well done, you good and faithful servant!' said his master, 'You have been faithful in managing small amounts, so I will put you in charge of large amounts. Come on in and share my happiness!' Then the servant who had received on thousand coins came in and said, 'Sir, I know you are a hard man; you reap harvests where you did not plant, and you gather crops where you did not scatter seed. I was afraid, so I went off and hid your money in the ground. Look! Here is what belongs to you.' 'You bad and lazy servant!' his master said. 'You knew, did you, that I reap harvests where I did not plant, and gather crops where I did not scatter seed? Well, then, you should have deposited my money in the bank, and I would have received it all back with interest when I returned. Now, take

the money away from him and give it to the one who has ten thousand coins. For to every person who has something, even more will be given, and he will have more than enough; but the person who has nothing, even the little that he has will be taken away from him. As for this useless servant—throw him outside in the darkness; there he will cry and gnash his teeth.'
Matthew 25: 14-30 GNB

Then he called the people to him, as well as his disciples, and said to them, 'Anyone who wishes to be a follower of mine must leave self behind; he must take up his cross, and come with me. Whoever cares for his own safety is lost; but if a man will let himself be lost for my sake and for the Gospel, that man is safe. What does a man gain by winning the whole world at the cost of his true self? What can he give to buy that self back? If anyone is ashamed of me and mine in this wicked and godless age, the Son of Man will be ashamed of him, when he comes in the glory of his Father and of the holy angels.
Mark 8: 34-38 NEB

"No one knows, however, when that day or hour will come—neither the angels in heaven, nor the Son; only the Father knows. Be on watch, be alert, for you do not know when the time will come. It will be like a man who goes away from home on a trip and leaves his servants in charge, after giving to each one his own work to do and after telling the doorkeeper to keep watch. Watch, then, because you do not know when the master of the house is coming—it might be in the evening or at midnight or before dawn or at sunrise. If he comes suddenly, he must not find you asleep. What I say to you, then, I say to all: Watch!" **Mark 13: 32-37 GNB**

And the multitudes asked him, "What then shall we do?" And he answered them, "He who has two coats, let him share with him who has none; and he who has food, let him do likewise." Tax collectors also came to be baptized, and said to him, "Teacher, what shall we do?" And he said to them, "Collect no more than is appointed you." Soldiers also asked him, "And we, what shall we do?" And he said to them, "Rob no one by violence or by false accusation, and be content with your wages."
Luke 3: 10-14 RSV

Then someone from the crowd said to him, "Teacher, tell my brother to divide the inheritance with me." But Jesus said to him, "Man, who made me a judge or arbitrator between you two?" Then he said to them, "Watch out and guard yourself from all types of greed, because one's life does not consist in the abundance of his possessions." He then told them a parable: "The land of a certain rich man produced an abundant crop, so he thought to himself, 'What should I do, for I have nowhere to store my crops?' Then he said, 'I will do this: I will tear down my barns and build bigger ones, and there I will store all my grain and my goods. And I will say to myself, "You have plenty of goods stored up for many years; relax, eat, drink, celebrate!"' But God said to him, 'You fool! This very night your life will be demanded back from you, but who will get what you have prepared for yourself?' So it is with the one who stores up riches for himself, but is not rich toward God."

Then Jesus said to his disciples, "Therefore I tell you, do not worry about your life, what you will eat, or about your body, what you will wear. For there is more to life than food, and more to the body than clothing. Consider the ravens: They do not sow or reap, they have no storeroom or barn, yet God feeds them. How much more valuable are you than the birds! And which of you by worrying can add an hour to his life? So if you cannot do such a very little thing as this, why do you worry about the rest? Consider how the flowers grow; they do not work or spin. Yet I tell you, not even Solomon in all his glory was clothed like one of these! And if this is how God clothes the wild grass, which is here today and tomorrow is tossed into the fire to heat the oven, how much more will he clothe you, you people of little faith! So do not be overly concerned about what you will eat and what you will drink, and do not worry about such things. For all the nations of the world pursue these things, and your Father knows that you need them. Instead, pursue his kingdom, and these things will be given to you as well.

"Do not be afraid, little flock, for your Father is well pleased to give you the kingdom. Sell your possessions and give to the poor. Provide yourselves purses that do not wear out – a treasure in heaven that never decreases, where no thief approaches and no moth destroys. For where your treasure is, there your heart will be also. **Luke 12: 13-34 NET***

"Salt is good, but if it loses its saltiness, how can it be made salty again? It is fit neither for the soil nor for the manure pile; it is thrown out. He who has ears to hear, let him hear." **Luke 14: 34-35 NIV**

Jesus also said to the disciples, "There was a rich man who was informed of accusations that his manager was wasting his assets. So he called the manager in and said to him, 'What is this I hear about you? Turn in the account of your administration, because you can no longer be my manager.' Then the manager said to himself, 'What should I do, since my master is taking my position away from me? I'm not strong enough to dig, and I'm too ashamed to beg. I know what to do so that when I am put out of management, people will welcome me into their homes.' So he contacted his master's debtors one by one. He asked the first, 'How much do you owe my master?' The man replied, 'A hundred measures of olive oil.' The manager said to him, 'Take your bill, sit down quickly, and write fifty.' Then he said to another, 'And how much do you owe?' The second man replied, 'A hundred measures of wheat.' The manager said to him, 'Take your bill, and write eighty.' The master commended the dishonest manager because he acted shrewdly. For the people of this world are more shrewd in dealing with their contemporaries than the people of light. And I tell you, make friends for yourselves by how you use worldly wealth, so that when it runs out you will be welcomed into the eternal homes.

"The one who is faithful in a very little is also faithful in much, and the one who is dishonest in a very little is also dishonest in much. If then you haven't been trustworthy in handling worldly wealth, who will entrust you with the true riches? And if you haven't been trustworthy with someone else's property, who will give you your own? No servant can serve two masters, for either he will hate the one and love the other, or he will be devoted to the one and despise the other. You cannot serve God and money."

The Pharisees (who loved money) heard all this and ridiculed him. But Jesus said to them, "You are the ones who justify yourselves in men's eyes, but God knows your hearts. For what is highly prized among men is utterly detestable in God's sight. **Luke 16: 1-15 NET~**

Jesus told his disciples, "It's inevitable that there will be causes for making bad decisions; but how sad it will be for any person who is responsible. It would be much better for him to be thrown into the ocean with a large anchor around his neck than for him to cause one of these little ones to go astray. Be careful about your example to others!" **Luke 17: 1-3 HOV**

For we see divine retribution revealed from heaven and falling upon all the godless wickedness of men. In their wickedness they are stifling the truth. For all that may be known of God by men lies plain before their eyes; indeed God himself has disclosed it to them. His invisible attributes, that is to say his everlasting power and deity, have been visible, ever since the world began, to the eye of reason, in the things he has made. There is therefore no possible defense for their conduct; knowing God, they have refused to honor him as God, or to render him thanks. Hence all their thinking has ended in futility, and their misguided minds are plunged in darkness. They boast of their wisdom, but they have made fools of themselves, exchanging the splendor of immortal God for an image shaped like mortal man, even for images like birds, beasts, and creeping things.

For this reason God has given them up to the vileness of their own desires, and the consequent degradation of their bodies, because they have bartered away the true God for a false one, and have offered reverence and worship to created things instead of to the Creator, who is blessed for ever; amen.

In consequence, I say, God has given them up to shameful passions. Their women have exchanged natural intercourse for unnatural, and their men in turn, giving up natural relations with women, burn with lust for one another; males behave indecently with males, and are paid in their own persons the fitting wage of such perversion.

Thus, because they have not seen fit to acknowledge God, he has given them up to their own depraved reason. This leads them to break all rules of conduct. They are filled with every kind of injustice, mischief, rapacity, and malice; they are one mass of envy, murder, rivalry, treachery, and malevolence; whisperers and scandal-mongers, hateful to God, insolent, arrogant, and boastful; they invent new kinds of mischief, they show no loyalty to parents, no conscience, no fidelity to their plighted word; they are without natural affection and without pity. They know well enough the just decree of God that those who behave like this deserve to die, and yet they do it; not only so, they actually applaud such practices.
Romans 1: 18-32 NEB

We know that the law is spiritual; but I am carnal, sold under sin. I do not understand my own actions. For I do not do what I want, but I do the very thing I hate. Now if I do what I do not want, I agree that the law is good. So then it is no longer I that do it, but sin which dwells within me. For I know that nothing good dwells within me, that is, in my flesh. I can will what is right, but I cannot do it. For I do not do the good I want, but the evil I do not want is what I do. Now if I do what I do not want, it is no longer I that do it, but sin which dwells within me.

So I find it to be a law that when I want to do right, evil lies close at hand. For I delight in the law of God, in my inmost self, but I see in my members another law at war with the law of my mind and making me captive to the law of sin which dwells in my members. Wretched man that I am! Who will deliver me from this body of death? Thanks be to God through Jesus Christ our Lord!
Romans 7: 14-25 RSV

And do this, understanding the present time. The hour has come for you to wake up from your slumber, because our salvation is nearer now than when we first believed. The night is nearly over; the day is almost here. So let us put aside the deeds of darkness and put on the armor of light. Let us behave decently, as in the daytime, not in orgies and drunkenness, not in sexual immorality and debauchery, not in dissension and jealousy. Rather, clothe yourselves with the Lord Jesus Christ, and do not think about how to gratify the desires of the sinful nature. Accept him whose faith is weak, without passing judgment on disputable matters.
Romans 13: 11- 14: 1 NIV

None of us lives or dies for self alone. If we live, we live for the Lord, and if we die we die for the Lord. Consequently, if we either live or die we are the Lord's. Christ died and rose from the grave in order that he

might be Lord of the dead and the living. So those of you who are vegetarians—why do you judge those who are not? And those of you who eat everything—why do you look down on your brothers and sisters? Obviously we all will be called before God as our judge.
Romans 14: 7-10 HOV

For none of us lives for himself and none dies for himself. If we live, we live for the Lord; if we die, we die for the Lord. Therefore, whether we live or die, we are the Lord's. For this reason Christ died and returned to life, so that he may be the Lord of both the dead and the living.

But you who eat vegetables only – why do you judge your brother or sister? And you who eat everything – why do you despise your brother or sister? For we will all stand before the judgment seat of God. **Romans 14: 7-10 NB**

Those of us who have a robust conscience must accept as our own burden the tender scruples of weaker men, and not consider ourselves. Each of us must consider his neighbor and think what is for his good and will build up the common life. For Christ too did not consider himself, but might have said, in the words of Scripture, 'The reproaches of those who reproach thee fell on me.' For all the ancient scriptures were written for our own instruction, in order that through the encouragement they give us we may maintain our hope with fortitude. And may God, the source of all fortitude and all encourage-ment, grant that you may agree with one another after the manner of Christ Jesus, so that with one mind and one voice you may praise the God and Father of our Lord Jesus Christ. In a word, accept one another as Christ accepted us, to the glory of God. **Romans 15: 1-7 NEB**

So, brothers and sisters, I could not speak to you as spiritual people, but instead as people of the flesh, as infants in Christ. I fed you milk, not solid food, for you were not yet ready. In fact, you are still not ready, for you are still influenced by the flesh. For since there is still jealousy and dissension among you, are you not influenced by the flesh and behaving like unregenerate people? For whenever someone says, "I am with Paul," or "I am with Apollos," are you not merely human?

What is Apollos, really? Or what is Paul? Servants through whom you came to believe, and each of us in the ministry the Lord gave us. I planted, Apollos watered, but God caused it to grow. So neither the one who plants counts for anything, nor the one who waters, but God who causes the growth. The one who plants and the one who waters work as one, but each will receive his reward according to his work. **I Corinthians 3: 1-8 NET**

"All things are lawful for me" – but not everything is beneficial. "All things are lawful for me" – but I will

not be controlled by anything. "Food is for the stomach and the stomach is for food, but God will do away with both." The body is not for sexual immorality, but for the Lord, and the Lord for the body. Now God indeed raised the Lord and he will raise us by his power. Do you not know that your bodies are members of Christ? Should I take the members of Christ and make them members of a prostitute? Never! Or do you not know that anyone who is united with a prostitute is one body with her? For it is said, "The two will become one flesh." But the one united with the Lord is one spirit with him. Flee sexual immorality! "Every sin a person commits is outside of the body" – but the immoral person sins against his own body. Or do you not know that your body is the temple of the Holy Spirit who is in you, whom you have from God, and you are not your own? For you were bought at a price. Therefore glorify God with your body.
I Corinthians 6: 12-20 NET

Be careful, however, not to let your freedom of action make those who are weak in the faith fall into sin. Suppose a person whose conscience is weak in this matter sees you, who have so-called "knowledge," eating in the temple of an idol; will not this encourage him to eat food offered to idols? And so this weak person, your brother for whom Christ died, will perish because of your "knowledge"! And in this way you will be sinning against Christ by sinning against your Christian brothers and wounding their weak conscience. So then,

if food makes my brother sin, I will never eat meat again, so as not to make my brother fall into sin.
I Corinthians 8: 9-13 GNB

So whether you eat or drink or whatever you do, do it all for the glory of God. Do not cause anyone to stumble, whether Jews, Greeks or the church of God—even as I try to please everybody in every way. For I am not seeking my own good but the good of many, so that they may be saved. **I Corinthians 10: 31-33 NIV**

Now the one who prepared us for this very purpose is God, who gave us the Spirit as a down payment. Therefore we are always full of courage, and we know that as long as we are alive here on earth we are absent from the Lord –for we live by faith, not by sight. Thus we are full of courage and would prefer to be away from the body and at home with the Lord. So then whether we are alive or away, we make it our ambition to please him. For we must all appear before the judgment seat of Christ, so that each one may be paid back according to what he has done while in the body, whether good or evil.

Therefore, because we know the fear of the Lord, we try to persuade people, but we are well known to God, and I hope we are well known to your consciences too. We are not trying to commend ourselves to you again, but are giving you an opportunity to be proud of us, so that you may be able to answer those who take pride in outward appearance and not in what is in the heart. For if we are out of our minds, it is for God; if we are of sound mind, it is for you. For the love of Christ controls us, since we have concluded this, that Christ died for all; therefore all have died. And he died for all so that those who live should no longer live for themselves but for him who died for them and was raised. So then from now on we acknowledge no one from an outward human point of view. Even though we have known Christ from such a human point of view, now we do not know him in that way any longer. So then, if anyone is in Christ, he is a new creation; what is old has passed away – look, what is new has come! And all these things are from God who reconciled us to himself through Christ, and who has given us the ministry of reconciliation. In other words, in Christ God was reconciling the world to himself, not counting people's trespasses against them, and he has given us the message of reconciliation. Therefore we are ambassadors for Christ, as though God were making His plea through us. We plead with you on Christ's behalf, "Be reconciled to God!" God made the one who did not know sin to be sin for us, so that in him we would become the righteousness of God. **II Corinthians 5: 5-21 NET**

If a man should do something wrong, my brothers, on a sudden impulse, you who are endowed with the Spirit must set him right again very gently. Look to yourself, each one of you: you may be tempted too. Help one another to carry these heavy loads, and in this way you will fulfill the law of Christ. For if a man imagines himself to be somebody, when he is nothing, he is deluding himself. Each man should examine his own conduct for himself; then he can measure his achievement by comparing himself with himself and not with anyone else. For everyone has his own proper burden to bear.

When anyone is under instruction in the faith, he should give his teacher a share of all good things he has. Make no mistake about this: God is not to be fooled; a man reaps what he sows. If he sows seed in the field of his lower nature, he will reap from it a harvest of corruption, but if he sows in the field of the Spirit, the Spirit will bring him a harvest of eternal life. So let us never tire of doing good, for if we do not slacken our efforts we shall in due time reap our harvest. Therefore, as opportunity offers, let us work for the good of all, especially members of the household of the faith. **Galatians 6: 1-10 NEB**

But that is not how you learned Christ. For were you not told of him, were you not as Christians taught the truth as it is in Jesus?—that, leaving your former way of life, you must lay aside that old human nature which deluded by its lusts, is sinking towards death. You must be made new in mind and spirit, and put on the new nature of God's creating, which shows itself in the just and devout life called for by the truth. Then throw off falsehood; speak the truth to each other, for all of us are the parts of one body. If you are angry, do not let anger lead you into sin; do not let sunset find you still nursing it; leave no loop-hole for the devil. The thief must give up stealing, and instead work hard and honestly with his own hands, so that he may have something to share with the needy.

No bad language must pass your lips, but only what is good and helpful to the occasion, so that it brings a blessing to those who hear it. And do not grieve the Holy Spirit of God, for that Spirit is the seal with which you were marked for the day of our final liberation. Have done with spite and passion, all angry shouting and cursing, and bad feeling of every kind. Be generous to one another, tender-hearted, forgiving one another as God in Christ forgave you. **Ephesians 4: 20-32 NEB**

Since you are God's dear children, you must try to be like him. Your life must be controlled by love, just as Christ loved us and gave his life for us as a sweet-smelling offering and sacrifice that pleases God.
Ephesians 5: 1-2 GNB

For you were once darkness, but now you are light in the Lord. Live as children of light (for the fruit of the light consists in all goodness, righteousness and truth) and find out what pleases the Lord. Have nothing to do with the fruitless deeds of darkness, but rather expose them. For it is shameful even to mention what the disobedient do in secret. But everything exposed by the light becomes visible, for it is light that makes everything visible. This is why it is said: "Wake up, O sleeper, rise from the dead, and Christ will shine on you." **Ephesians 5: 8-13 NIV**

Wives, submit to your husbands as to the Lord, because the husband is the head of the wife as also Christ is the head of the church – he himself being the savior of the body. But as the church submits to Christ, so also wives should submit to their husbands in everything.

Husbands, love your wives just as Christ loved the church and gave himself for her to sanctify her by cleansing her with the washing of the water by the word, so that he may present the church to himself as glorious – not having a stain or wrinkle, or any such blemish, but holy and blameless. In the same way husbands ought to love their wives as their own bodies. He who loves his wife loves himself. For no one has ever hated his own body but he feeds it and takes care of it, just as Christ also does the church, for we are members of his body. For this reason a man will leave his father and mother and will be joined to his wife, and the two will become one flesh. This mystery is great – but I am actually speaking with reference to Christ and the church. Nevertheless, each one of you must also love his own wife as he loves himself, and the wife must respect her husband. **Ephesians 5: 22-33 NET**

In my life in union with the Lord it is a great joy to me that after so long a time you once more had the chance

of showing that you care for me. I don't mean that you had stopped caring for me—you just had no chance to show it. And I am not saying this because I feel neglected, for I have learned to be satisfied with what I have. I know what it is to be in need and what it is to have more than enough. I have learned this secret, so that anywhere, at any time, I am content, whether I am full or hungry, whether I have too much or too little. I have the strength to face all conditions by the power that Christ gives me.
Philippians 4: 10-13 GNB

For this reason we have always prayed for you, ever since we heard about you. We ask God to fill you with the knowledge of his will, with all the wisdom and understanding that his Spirit gives. Then you will be able to live as the Lord wants and will always do what pleases him. Your lives will produce all kinds of good deeds, and you will grow in your knowledge of God. May you be made strong with all the strength which comes from his glorious power, so that you may be able to endure everything with patience. And with joy give thanks to the Father, who has made you fit to have your share of what God has reserved for his people in the kingdom of light. He rescued us from the power of darkness and brought us safe into the kingdom of his dear Son, by whom we are set free, that is, our sins are forgiven.
Colossians 1: 9-14 GNB

Put on then, as God's chosen ones, holy and beloved, compassion, kindness, lowliness, meekness, and patience, forbearing one another and, if one has a complaint against another, forgiving each other; as the Lord has forgiven you, so you also must forgive. And above all these put on love, which binds everything together in perfect harmony. And let the peace of Christ rule in your hearts, to which indeed you were called in the one body. And be thankful. Let the word of Christ dwell in you richly, as you teach and admonish one another in all wisdom, and as you sing psalms and hymns and spiritual songs with thankfulness in your hearts to God. And whatever you do, in word or deed, do everything in the name of the Lord Jesus, giving thanks to God the Father through him.
Colossians 3: 12-17 RSV~

But as to the times and the seasons, brethren, you have no need to have anything written to you. For you yourselves know well that the day of the Lord will come like a thief in the night. When people say, "There is peace and security," then sudden destruction will come upon them as travail comes upon a woman with child, and there will be no escape. But you are not in darkness, brethren, for that day to surprise you like a thief. For you are all sons of light and sons of the day; we are not of the night or of darkness. So then let us not sleep, as others do, but let us keep awake and be sober. For those who sleep sleep at night, and those who get drunk are drunk at night. But, since we belong to the day, let us be sober and put on the breastplate of faith and love, and for a helmet the hope of salvation. For God has not destined us for wrath, but to obtain salvation through our Lord Jesus Christ, who died for us so that whether we wake or sleep we might live with him. Therefore encourage one another and build one another up, just as you are doing.

But we beseech you, brethren, to respect those who labor among you and are over you in the Lord and admonish you, and to esteem them very highly in love because of their work. Be at peace among yourselves. And we exhort you, brethren, admonish the idle, encourage the fainthearted, help the weak, be patient with them all. See that none of you repays evil for evil, but always seek to do good to one another and to all. Rejoice always, pray constantly, give thanks in all circumstances; for this is the will of God in Christ Jesus for you. Do not quench the Spirit, do not despise prophesying, but test everything; hold fast what is good, abstain from every form of evil.
I Thessalonians 5: 1-22 RSV

Well, religion does make a person very rich, if he is satisfied with what he has. What did we bring into the world? Nothing! What can we take out of the world? Nothing! So then, if we have food and clothes, that should be enough for us. But those who want to get rich fall into temptation and are caught in the trap of many foolish and harmful desires, which pull them down to ruin and destruction. For the love of money is a source of all kinds of evil. Some have been so eager to have it that they have wandered away from the faith and have broken their hearts with many sorrows.

But you, man of God, avoid all these things. Strive for righteousness, godliness, faith, love, endurance, and gentleness. Run your best in the race of faith, and win eternal life for yourself; for it was to this life that God called you when you firmly professed your faith before many witnesses. Before God, who gives life to all things, and before Christ Jesus, who firmly professed his faith before Pontius Pilate, I command you to obey your orders and keep them faithfully until the Day when our Lord Jesus Christ will appear. His appearing will be brought about at the right time by God, the blessed and only Ruler, the King of kings and the Lord of lords. He alone is immortal; he lives in the light that no one can approach. No one has ever seen him. To him be honor and eternal power! Amen.

Command those who are rich in the things of this life not to be proud, but to place their hope, not in such an uncertain thing as riches, but in God, who generously gives us everything for our enjoyment. Command them to do good, to be rich in good works, to be generous and ready to share with others. In this way they will store up for themselves a treasure which will be a solid foundation for the future. And then they will be able to win the life which is true life. **I Timothy 6: 6-19 GNB**

Endure hardship as discipline; God is treating you as sons. For what son is not disciplined by his father? If you are not disciplined (and everyone undergoes discipline), then you are illegitimate children and not true sons. Moreover, we have all had human fathers who disciplined us and we respected them for it. How much more should we submit to the Father of our spirits and live! Our fathers disciplined us for a little while as they thought best; but God disciplines us for our good, that we may share in his holiness. No discipline seems pleasant at the time, but painful. Later on, however, it produces a harvest of righteousness and peace for those who have been trained by it. **Hebrews 12: 7-11 NIV**

Let brotherly love continue. Do not neglect to show hospitality to strangers, for thereby some have entertained angels unawares. Remember those who are in prison, as though in prison with them; and those who are ill-treated, since you also are in the body. Let marriage be held in honor among all, and let the marriage bed be undefiled; for God will judge the immoral and adulterous. Keep your life free from love of money, and be content with what you have; for he has said, "I will never fail you nor forsake you." Hence we can confidently say, "The Lord is my helper, I will not be afraid; what can man do to me?" **Hebrews 13: 1-6 RSV**

The Christian who is poor must be glad when God lifts him up, and the rich Christian must be glad when God brings him down. **James 1: 9-10 GNB**

Do not be deceived, my dear brothers! Every good gift and every perfect present comes from heaven; it comes down from God, the Creator of the heavenly lights, who does not change or cause darkness by turning. By his own will he brought us into being through the word of truth, so that we should have first place among all this creatures.

Remember this, my dear brothers! Everyone must be quick to listen, but slow to speak and slow to become angry. Man's anger does not achieve God's righteous purpose. So get rid of every filthy habit and all wicked conduct. Submit to God and accept the word that he plants in your hearts, which is able to save you.

Do not deceive yourselves by just listening to his word; instead, put it into practice. Whoever listens to the word but does not put it into practice is like a man who looks in a mirror and sees himself as he is. He takes a good look at himself and then goes away and at once forgets what he looks like. But whoever looks closely into the perfect law that sets people free, who keeps on paying attention to it and does not simply listen and then forget it, but puts it into practice—that person will be blessed by God in what he does.

Does anyone think he is religious? If he does not control his tongue, his religion is worthless and he deceives himself. What God the Father considers to be pure and genuine religion is this: to take care of orphans and widows in their suffering and to keep oneself from being corrupted by the world. **James 1: 16-27 GNB**

Is there anyone among you who is wise and understanding? He is to prove it by his good life, by his good deeds performed with humility and wisdom. But if in your heart you are jealous, bitter, and selfish, don't sin against the truth by boasting of your wisdom. Such wisdom does not come down from heaven; it belongs to the world, it is unspiritual and demonic. Where there is jealousy and selfishness, there is also disorder and every kind of evil. But the wisdom from above is pure first of all; it is also peaceful, gentle, and friendly; it is full of compassion and produces a harvest of good deeds; it is free from prejudice and hypocrisy. And goodness is the harvest that is produced from the seeds the peacemakers plant in peace. **James 3: 13-18 GNB**

Be patient, then, brothers, until the Lord's coming. See how the farmer waits for the land to yield its valuable crop and how patient he is for the autumn and spring rains. You too, be patient and stand firm, because the Lord's coming is near. Don't grumble against each other, brothers, or you will be judged. The Judge is standing at the door! Brothers, as an example of patience in the face of suffering, take the prophets who spoke in the name of the Lord. As you know, we consider blessed those who have persevered. You have heard of Job's perseverance and have seen what the Lord finally brought about. The Lord is full of compassion and mercy.
James 5: 7-11 NIV

Who will harm you if you are eager to do what is good?

But even if you should suffer for doing what is right, how happy you are! Do not be afraid of anyone, and do not worry. But have reverence for Christ in your hearts, and honor him as Lord. Be ready at all times to answer anyone who asks you to explain the hope you have in you, but do it with gentleness and respect. Keep your conscience clear, so that when you are insulted, those who speak evil of your good conduct as followers of Christ will become ashamed of what they say. For it is better to suffer for doing good, if this should be God's will, than for doing evil. For Christ died for sins once and for all, a good man on behalf of sinners, in order to lead you to God. **I Peter 3: 13-18 GNB**

If we obey God's commands, then we are sure that we know him. If someone says that he knows him, but does not obey his commands, such a person is a liar and there is no truth in him. But whoever obeys his word is the one whose love for God has really been made perfect. This is how we can be sure that we are in union with God: whoever says that he remains in union with God should live just as Jesus Christ did. **I John 2: 3-6 GNB**

Whoever says that he is in the light, yet hates his brother, is in the darkness to this very hour. Whoever loves his brother lives in the light, and so there is nothing in him that will cause someone else to sin. **I John 2: 9-10 GNB**

Do not love the world or anything that belongs to the world. If you love the world, you do not love the Father.

Everything that belongs to the world—what the sinful self desires, what people see and want, and everything in this world that people are so proud of—none of this comes from the Father; it all comes from the world. The world and everything in it that people desire is passing away; but he who does the will of God lives forever.
I John 2: 15-17 GNB

WORSHIP

O LORD, our Lord, how majestic is your name in all the earth! You have set your glory above the heavens. From the lips of children and infants you have ordained praise because of your enemies, to silence the foe and the avenger. When I consider your heavens, the work of your fingers, the moon and the stars, which you have set in place, what is man that you are mindful of him, the son of man that you care for him? You made him a little lower than the heavenly beings and crowned him with glory and honor. You made him ruler over the works of your hands; you put everything under his feet: all flocks and herds, and the beasts of the field, the birds of the air, and the fish of the sea, all that swim the paths of the seas. O LORD, our Lord, how majestic is your name in all the earth! **Psalms 8: 1-9 NIV**

The earth is the Lord's and the fullness thereof, the world and those who dwell therein; for he has founded it upon the seas, and established it upon the rivers. Who shall ascend the hill of the Lord? And who shall stand in his holy place? He who has clean hands and

a pure heart, who does not lift up his soul to what is false, and does not swear deceitfully. He will receive blessing from the Lord, and vindication from the God of his salvation. Such is the generation of those who seek him, who seek the face of the God of Jacob. Lift up your heads, O gates! And be lifted up, O ancient doors! That the King of glory may come in. Who is the King of glory? The Lord, strong and mighty, the Lord, mighty in battle! Lift up your heads, O gates! And be lifted up, O ancient doors! That the King of glory may come in! Who is this King of glory? The Lord of hosts, he is the King of glory!
Psalm 24: 1-10 RSV

O come, let us sing to the Lord; let us make a joyful noise to the rock of our salvation! Let us come into his presence with thanksgiving; let us make a joyful noise to him with songs of praise! For the Lord is a great God, and a great King above all gods. In his hand are the depths of the earth; the heights of the mountains are his also. The sea is his, for he made it; for his hands formed the dry land. O come, let us worship and bow down, let us kneel before the Lord, our Maker! For he is our God, and we are the people of is pasture, and the sheep of his hand. **Psalm 95: 1-7 RSV~**

Make a joyful noise to the Lord, all the lands! Serve the Lord with gladness! Come into his presence with singing! Know that the Lord is God! It is he that made us, and we are his; we are his people, and the sheep of his pasture. Enter his gates with thanksgiving, and his courts with praise! Give thanks to him, bless his name! For the Lord is good; his steadfast love endures for ever, and his faithfulness to all generations. **Psalms 100: 1-5 RSV+**

You Samaritans worship without knowing what you worship, while we worship what we know. It is from the Jews that salvation comes. But the time approaches, indeed it is already here, when those who are real worshippers will worship the Father in spirit and in truth. Such are the worshippers whom the Father wants. God is spirit, and those who worship him must worship in spirit and in truth.' **John 4: 22-24 NEB**

So Paul stood before the Areopagus and said, "Men of Athens, I see that you are very religious in all respects. For as I went around and observed closely your objects of worship, I even found an altar with this inscription: 'To an unknown god.' Therefore what you worship without knowing it, this I proclaim to you. The God who made the world and everything in it, who is Lord of heaven and earth, does not live in temples made by human hands, nor is he served by human hands, as if he needed anything, because he himself gives life and breath and everything to everyone. From one man he made every nation of the human race to inhabit the entire earth, determining their set times and the fixed limits of the places where they would live, so that they would search for God and perhaps grope around for him and find him, though he is not far from each one of us. For in him we live and move about and exist, as even some of your own poets have said, 'For we too are his offspring.' So since we are God's offspring, we should not think the deity is like gold or silver or stone, an image made by human skill and imagination. Therefore, although God has overlooked such times of ignorance, he now commands all people everywhere to repent, because he has set a day on which he is going to judge the world in righteousness, by a man whom he designated, having provided proof to everyone by raising him from the dead." **Acts 17: 22-31 NET**

Oh, the depth of the riches of the wisdom and knowledge of God! How unsearchable his judgments, and his paths beyond tracing out! Who has known the mind of the Lord? Or who has been his counselor? Who has ever given to God, that God should repay him? For from him and through him and to him are all things. To him be the glory forever! Amen.

Therefore, I urge you, brothers, in view of God's mercy, to offer your bodies as living sacrifices, holy and pleasing to God—this is your spiritual act of worship. Do not conform any longer to the pattern of this world, but be transformed by the renewing of your mind. Then you will be able to test and approve what God's will is—his good, pleasing and perfect will. **Romans 11: 33- 12: 2 NIV**

For I received from the Lord what I also passed on to you, that the Lord Jesus on the night in which he was betrayed took bread, and after he had given thanks he broke it and said, "This is my body, which is for you. Do this in remembrance of me." In the same way, he also took the cup after supper, saying, "This cup is the new covenant in my blood. Do this, every time you drink it, in remembrance of me." For every time you eat this bread and drink the cup, you proclaim the Lord's death until he comes.

For this reason, whoever eats the bread or drinks the cup of the Lord in an unworthy manner will be guilty of the body and blood of the Lord. A person should examine himself first, and in this way let him eat the bread and drink of the cup. For the one who eats and drinks without careful regard for the body eats and drinks judgment against himself. **I Corinthians 11: 23-29 NET**

Praise be to the God and Father of our Lord Jesus Christ, who has bestowed on us in Christ every spiritual blessing in the heavenly realms. In Christ he chose us before the world was founded, to be dedicated, to be without blemish in his sight, to be full of love; and he destined us—such was his will and pleasure—to be accepted as his sons through Jesus Christ, that the glory of his gracious gift, so graciously bestowed on us in his Beloved, might redound to his praise. For in Christ our release is secured and our sins are forgiven through the shedding of his blood. Therein lies the richness of God's free grace lavished upon us, imparting full wisdom and insight. He has made known to us his hidden purpose—such was his will and pleasure determined beforehand in Christ—to be put into effect when the time was ripe: namely, that the universe, all in heaven and on earth, might be brought into a unity in Christ.

In Christ indeed we have been given our share in the heritage, as was decreed in his design whose purpose is everywhere at work. For it was his will that we, who were the first to set our hope on Christ, should cause his glory to be praised. And you too, when you had heard the message of the truth, the good news of your salvation, and had believed it, became incorporate in Christ and received the seal of the promised Holy Spirit; and that Spirit is the pledge that we shall enter upon our heritage, when God has redeemed what is his own, to his praise and glory. **Ephesians 1: 3-14 NEB**

First of all, then, I urge that petitions, prayers, requests, and thanksgivings be offered to God for all people; for kings and all others who are in authority, that we may live a quiet and peaceful life with all reverence toward God and with proper conduct. This is good and it pleases God our Savior, who wants everyone to be saved and to come to know the truth. For there is one God, and there is one who brings God and mankind together, the man Christ Jesus, who gave himself to redeem all mankind. That was the proof at the right time that God wants everyone to be saved, and that is why I was sent as an apostle and teacher of the Gentiles, to proclaim the message of faith and truth. I am not lying; I am telling the truth! In every church service I want the men to pray, men who are dedicated to God and can lift up their hands in prayer without anger or argument. **I Timothy 2: 1-8 GNB**

Therefore, since we are receiving a kingdom that cannot be shaken, let us be thankful, and so worship God acceptably with reverence and awe, for our "God is a consuming fire." **Hebrews 12: 28-29 NIV**

Now may the God of peace who brought again from the dead our Lord Jesus, the great shepherd of the sheep, by the blood of the eternal covenant, equip you with everything good that you may do his will, working in you that which is pleasing in his sight, through Jesus Christ; to whom be glory for ever and ever. Amen. **Hebrews 13: 20-21 RSV**

Baptism / Confession

Blessed is he whose transgression is forgiven, whose sin is covered. Blessed is the man to whom the Lord imputes no iniquity, and in whose spirit there is no deceit. When I declared not my sin, my body wasted away through my groaning all day long. For day and night thy hand was heavy upon me; my strength was dried up as by the heat of summer. I acknowledged my sin to thee, and I did not hide my iniquity; I said, "I will confess my transgressions to the Lord"; then thou didst forgive the guilt of my sin. **Psalms 32:1-5 RSV**

Have mercy on me, O God, according to thy steadfast love; according to thy abundant mercy blot out my transgressions. Wash me thoroughly from my iniquity, and cleanse me from my sin! For I know my transgressions, and my sin is ever before me. Against thee, thee only, have I sinned, and done that which is evil in thy sight, so that thou art justified in thy sentence and blameless in thy judgment. Behold, I was brought forth in iniquity, and in sin did my mother conceive me. Behold, thou desirest truth in the inward being; therefore teach me wisdom in my secret heart. Purge me with hyssop, and I shall be clean; wash me, and I shall be whiter than snow. Fill me with joy and gladness; let the bones which thou hast broken rejoice. Hide thy face from my sins, and blot out all my iniquities.

Create in me a clean heart, O God, and put a new and right spirit within me. Caste me not away from thy presence, and take not thy holy Spirit from me. Restore to me the joy of thy salvation, and uphold me with a willing spirit. Then I will teach transgressors thy ways, and sinners will return to thee. Deliver me from bloodguiltiness, O God, thou God of my salvation, and my tongue will sing aloud of thy deliverance.

O Lord, open thou my lips, and my mouth shall show forth thy praise. For thou hast no delight in sacrifice; were I to give a burnt offering, thou wouldst not be pleased. The sacrifice acceptable to God is a broken spirit; a broken and contrite heart, O God, thou wilt not despise. **Psalm 51: 1-17 RSV+**

"And now, my brothers, I know that what you and your leaders did to Jesus was due to your ignorance. God announced long ago through all the prophets that his Messiah had to suffer; and he made it come true in this way. Repent, then, and turn to God, so that he will forgive your sins. If you do, times of spiritual strength will come from the Lord, and he will send Jesus, who is the Messiah he has already chosen for you. He must remain in heaven until the time comes for all things to be made new, as God announced through his holy prophets of long ago. For Moses said, 'The Lord your God will send you a prophet, just as he sent me, and he will be one of your own people. You are to obey everything that he tells you to do. **Acts 3: 17-22 GNB**

What are we to say, then? Shall we persist in sin, so that there may be all the more grace? No, no! We died to sin: how can we live in it any longer? Have you forgotten that when we were baptized into union with Christ Jesus we were baptized into his death? By baptism we were buried with him, and lay dead, in order that, as Christ was raised from the dead in the splendor of the Father, so also we might set our feet upon the new path of life.

For if we have become incorporate with him in a death like his, we shall also be one with him in a resurrection like his. We know that the man we once were has been crucified with Christ, for the destruction of the sinful self, so that we may no longer be the slaves of sin, since a dead man is no longer answerable for his sin. But if we thus died with Christ, we believe that we shall also come to life with him. We know that Christ, once raised from the dead, is never to die again: he is no longer under the dominion of death. For in dying as he did, he died to sin, once for all, and in living as he lives, he lives to God. In the same way you must regard yourselves as dead to sin and alive to God, in union with Christ Jesus.

Romans 6: 1-11 NEB+

In union with Christ you were circumcised, not with the circumcision that is made by men, but with the circumcision made by Christ, which consists of being freed from the power of this sinful self. For when you were baptized, you were buried with Christ, and in baptism you were also raised with Christ through your faith in the active power of God, who raised him from death. You were at one time spiritually dead because of your sins and because you were Gentiles without the Law. But God has now brought you to life with Christ. God forgave us all our sins; he canceled the unfavorable record of our debts with its binding rules and did away with it completely by nailing it to the cross. And on that cross Christ freed himself from the power of the spiritual rulers and authorities; he made a public spectacle of them by leading them as captives in his victory procession.

Colossians 2: 11-15 GNB

For the word of God is living and active, sharper than any two-edged sword, piercing to the division of soul and spirit, of joints and marrow, and discerning the thoughts and intentions of the heart. And before him no creature is hidden, but all are open and laid bare to the eyes of him with whom we have to do.

Since then we have a great high priest who has passed through the heavens, Jesus, the Son of God, let us hold fast our confession. For we have not a high priest who is unable to sympathize with our weaknesses, but one who in every respect has been tempted as we are, yet without sinning. Let us then with confidence draw near to the throne of grace, that we may receive mercy and find grace to help in time of need. **Hebrews 4: 14-16 RSV**

Therefore, brethren, since we have confidence to enter the sanctuary by the blood of Jesus, by the new and living way which he opened for us through the curtain, that is, through his flesh, and since we have a great high priest over the house of God, let us draw near with a true heart in full assurance of faith, with our hearts sprinkled clean from an evil conscience and our bodies washed with pure water. Let us hold fast the confession of our hope without wavering, for he who promised is faithful; and let us consider how to stir up one another to love and good works, not neglecting to meet together, as is the habit of some, but encouraging one another, and all the more as you see the Day drawing near. **Hebrews 10: 19-25 RSV**

Now the message that we have heard from his Son and announce is this: God is light, and there is no darkness at all in him. If, then, we say that we have fellowship with him, yet at the same time live in the darkness, we are lying both in our words and in our actions. But if we live in the light—just as he is in the light—then we have fellowship with one another, and the blood of Jesus, his Son, purifies us from every sin.

If we say that we have no sin, we deceive ourselves, and there is no truth in us. But if we confess our sins to God, he will keep his promise and do what is right: he will forgive us our sins and purify us from all our wrongdoing. If we say that we have not sinned, we make a liar out of God, and his word is not in us. **I John 1: 5-10 GNB+**

GRACE / FORGIVENESS

Then Peter came to Jesus and asked, "Lord, if my brother keeps on sinning against me, how many times do I have to forgive him? Seven times?" "No, not seven times," answered Jesus, "but seventy times seven, because the Kingdom of heaven is like this. Once there was a king who decided to check on his servants' accounts. He had just begun to do so when one of them was brought in who owed him millions of dollars. The servant did not have enough to pay is debt, so the king ordered him to be sold as a slave, with his wife and his children and all that he had, in order to pay the debt. The servant fell on his knees before the king. 'Be patient with me,' he begged, 'and I will pay you everything!' The king felt sorry for him, so he forgave him the debt and let him go.

Then the man went out and met one of his fellow servants who owed him a few dollars. He grabbed him and started choking him. 'Pay back what you owe me!' he said. His fellow servant fell down and begged him, 'Be patient with me, and I will pay you back!' But he refused; instead, he had him thrown into jail until he should pay the debt. When the other servants saw what had happened, they were very upset and went to the king and told him everything. So he called the servant in. 'You worthless slave!' he said. 'I forgave you the whole amount you owed me, just because you asked me to. You should have had mercy on your fellow servant, just as I had mercy on you.' The king was very angry, and he sent the servant to jail to be punished until he should pay back the whole amount." And Jesus concluded, "That is how my Father in heaven will treat every one of you unless you forgive your brother from your heart." **Matthew 18: 21-35 GNB**

So watch yourselves. "If your brother sins, rebuke him, and if he repents, forgive him. If he sins against you seven times in a day, and seven times comes back to you and says, 'I repent,' forgive him." **Luke 17: 3-4 NIV**

But God's act of grace is out of all proportion to Adam's wrongdoing. For if the wrongdoing of that one man brought death upon so many, its effect is vastly exceeded by the grace of God and the gift that came to so many by the grace of the one man, Jesus Christ. And again, the gift of God is not to be compared in its effect with that one man's sin; for the judicial action, following upon the one offence, issued in a verdict of condemnation, but the act of grace, following upon so many misdeeds, issued in a verdict of acquittal. For if by the wrongdoing of that one man death established its reign, through a single sinner, much more shall those who receive in far greater measure God's grace, and his gift of righteousness, live and reign through the one man, Jesus Christ.

It follows, then, that as the issue of one misdeed was condemnation for all men, so the issue of one just act is acquittal and life for all men. For as through the disobedience of the one man the many were made sinners, so through the obedience of the one man the many will be made righteous. Law intruded into this process to multiply law-breaking. But where sin was thus multiplied, grace immeasurably exceeded it, in order that, as sin established its reign by the way of death, so God's grace might establish its reign in righteousness, and issue in eternal life through Jesus Christ our Lord.
Romans 5: 15-21 NEB

His choice is based on his grace, not on what they have done. For it God's choice were based on what people do, then his grace would not be real grace.
Romans 11: 6 GNB

God has shown that all people are rebellious and sinful; consequently, he is able to show mercy and forgiveness to the whole human race. **Romans 11: 32 HOV**

But if anyone has caused sadness, he has not saddened me alone, but to some extent (not to exaggerate) he has saddened all of you as well. This punishment on such an individual by the majority is enough for him, so that now instead you should rather forgive and comfort him. This will keep him from being overwhelmed by excessive grief to the point of despair. Therefore I urge you to reaffirm your love for him. For this reason also I wrote you: to test you to see if you are obedient in everything. If you forgive anyone for anything, I also forgive him – for indeed what I have forgiven (if I have forgiven anything) I did so for you in the presence of Christ, so that we may not be exploited by Satan (for we are not ignorant of his schemes). **II Corinthians 2: 5-11 NET**

Time was when you were dead in your sins and wickedness, when you followed the evil ways of this present age, when you obeyed the commander of the spiritual powers of the air, the spirit now at work among God's rebel subjects. We too were of their number: we all lived our lives in sensuality, and obeyed the promptings of our own instincts and notions. In our natural condition we, like the rest, lay under the dreadful judgment of God. But God, rich in mercy, for the great love he bore us, brought us to life with Christ even when we were dead in our sins; it is by his grace you are saved. And in union with Christ Jesus he raised us up and enthroned us with him in the heavenly realms, so that he might display in the ages to come how immense are the resources of his grace, and how great his kindness to us in Christ Jesus. For it is by his grace you are saved, through trusting him; it is not your own doing. It is God's gift, not a reward for work done. There is nothing for anyone to boast of. For we are God's handiwork, created in Christ Jesus to devote ourselves to the good deeds for which God has designed us. **Ephesians 2: 1-10 NEB+**

I give thanks to Christ Jesus our Lord, who has given me strength for my work. I thank him for considering me worthy and appointing me to serve him, even though in the past I spoke evil of him and persecuted and insulted him. But God was merciful to me because I did not yet have faith and so did not know what I was doing. And our Lord poured out his abundant grace on me and gave me the faith and love which are ours in union with Christ Jesus. This is a true saying, to be completely accepted and believed: Christ Jesus came into the world to save sinners. I am the worst of them, but God was merciful to me in order that Christ Jesus might show his full patience in dealing with me, the worst of sinners, as an example for all those who would later believe in him and receive eternal life. To the eternal King, immortal and invisible, the only God—to him be honor and glory forever and ever! Amen. **I Timothy 1: 12-17 GNB**

I am writing this to you, my children, so that you will not sin; but if anyone does sin, we have someone who pleads with the Father on our behalf—Jesus Christ, the righteous one. And Christ himself is the means by which our sins are forgiven, and not our sins only, but also the sins of everyone. **I John 2: 1-2 GNB**

CHANGE

This is the word that came to Jeremiah from the LORD: "Stand at the gate of the LORD's house and there proclaim this message: 'Hear the word of the LORD, all you people of Judah who come through these gates to worship the LORD.' This is what the LORD Almighty, the God of Israel, says: "Reform your ways and your actions, and I will let you live in this place. Do not trust in deceptive words and say, 'This is the temple of the LORD, the temple of the LORD, the temple of the LORD!' If you really change your ways and your actions and deal with each other justly, if you do not oppress the alien, the fatherless or the widow and do not shed innocent blood in this place, and if you do not follow other gods to your own harm, then I will let you live in this place, in the land I gave your forefathers for ever and ever. But look, you are trusting in deceptive words that are worthless. Will you steal and murder, commit adultery and perjury, burn incense to Baal and follow other gods you have not known, and then come and stand before me in this house, which bears my Name, and say, 'We are safe'—safe to do all these detestable things? Has this house, which bears my Name, become a den of robbers to you? But I have been watching!" declares the LORD. **Jeremiah 7: 1-11 NIV**

"What do you think? There was a man who had two sons. He went to the first and said, 'Son, go and work today in the vineyard.' 'I will not,' he answered, but later he changed his mind and went. Then the father went to the other son and said the same thing. He answered, 'I will, sir,' but he did not go. Which of the two did what his father wanted?" "The first," they answered. Jesus said to them, "I tell you the truth, the tax collectors and the prostitutes are entering the kingdom of God ahead of you. For John came to you to show you the way of righteousness, and you did not believe him, but the tax collectors and the prostitutes did. And even after you saw this, you did not repent and believe him.
Matthew 21: 28-32 NIV

Jesus went on to say, "The Kingdom of God is like this. A man scatters seed in his field. He sleeps at night, is up and about during the day, and all the while the seeds are sprouting and growing. Yet he does not know how it happens. The soil itself makes the plants grow and bear fruit; first the tender stalk appears, then the head, and finally the head full of grain. When the grain is ripe, the man starts cutting it with his sickle, because harvest time has come.

"What shall we say the Kingdom of God is like?" asked

Jesus. "What parable shall we use to explain it? It is like this. A man takes a mustard seed, the smallest seed in the world, and plants it in the ground. After a while it grows up and becomes the biggest of all plants. It puts out such large branches that the birds come and make their nests in its shade." **Mark 4: 26-32 GNB**

Now there were some present on that occasion who told him about the Galileans whose blood Pilate had mixed with their sacrifices. He answered them, "Do you think these Galileans were worse sinners than all the other Galileans, because they suffered these things? No, I tell you! But unless you repent, you will all perish as well! Or those eighteen who were killed when the tower in Siloam fell on them, do you think they were worse offenders than all the others who live in Jerusalem? No, I tell you! But unless you repent you will all perish as well!" **Luke 13: 1-5 NET**

So Jesus told them this parable: "Which one of you, if he has a hundred sheep and loses one of them, would not leave the ninety-nine in the open pasture and go look for the one that is lost until he finds it? Then when he has found it, he places it on his shoulders, rejoicing. Returning home, he calls together his friends and neighbors, telling them, 'Rejoice with me, because I have found my sheep that was lost.' I tell you, in the same way there will be more joy in heaven over one sinner who repents than over ninety-nine righteous people who have no need to repent.

"Or what woman, if she has ten silver coins and loses one of them, does not light a lamp, sweep the house, and search thoroughly until she finds it? Then when she has found it, she calls together her friends and neighbors, saying, 'Rejoice with me, for I have found the coin that I had lost.' In the same way, I tell you, there is joy in the presence of God's angels over one sinner who repents."

Then Jesus said, "A man had two sons. The younger of them said to his father, 'Father, give me the share of the estate that will belong to me.' So he divided his assets between them. After a few days, the younger son gathered together all he had and left on a journey to a distant country, and there he squandered his wealth with a wild lifestyle. Then after he had spent everything, a severe famine took place in that country, and he began to be in need. So he went and worked for one of the citizens of that country, who sent him to his fields to feed pigs. He was longing to eat the carob pods the pigs were eating, but no one gave him anything. But when he came to his senses he said, 'How many of my father's hired workers have food enough to spare, but here I am dying from hunger! I will get up and go to my father and say to him, "Father, I have sinned against heaven and against you. I am no longer worthy to be called your son; treat me like one of your hired workers."' So he got up and went to his father. But while he was still a long way from home his father saw him, and his heart went out to him; he ran and hugged his son and kissed him. Then his son said to him, 'Father, I have sinned against heaven and against you; I am no longer worthy to be called your son.' But the father said to his slaves, 'Hurry! Bring the best robe, and put it on him! Put a ring on his finger and sandals on his feet! Bring the fattened calf and kill it! Let us eat and celebrate, because this son of mine was dead, and is alive again – he was lost and is found!' So they began to celebrate.

"Now his older son was in the field. As he came and approached the house, he heard music and dancing. So he called one of the slaves and asked what was happening. The slave replied, 'Your brother has returned, and your father has killed the fattened calf because he got his son back safe and sound.' But the older son became angry and refused to go in. His father came out and appealed to him, but he answered his father, 'Look! These many years I have worked like a slave for you, and I never disobeyed your commands. Yet you never gave me even a goat so that I could celebrate with my friends!
But when this son of yours came back, who has devoured your assets with prostitutes, you killed the fattened calf for him!'

Then the father said to him, 'Son, you are always with me, and everything that belongs to me is yours. It was appropriate to celebrate and be glad, for your brother was dead, and is alive; he was lost and is found.'"
Luke 15: 3-32 NET*

Don't be conformed to the standards of the world, but be transformed by a complete change of your mind. Then you will be able to understand the will of God—what is good and pleasing and perfect in his sight. **Romans 12: 2 HOV**

Listen, I will tell you a mystery: We will not all sleep, but we will all be changed –in a moment, in the blinking of an eye, at the last trumpet. For the trumpet will sound, and the dead will be raised imperishable, and we will be changed. For this perishable body must put on the imperishable, and this mortal body must put on immortality. Now when this perishable puts on the imperishable, and this mortal puts on immortality, then the saying that is written will happen, "Death has been swallowed up in victory." **I Corinthians 15: 51-54 NET**

Even if I did wound you by the letter I sent, I do not now regret it. I may have been sorry for it when I saw that the letter had caused you pain, even if only for a time; but now I am happy, not that your feelings were wounded but that the wound led to a change of heart. You bore the smart as God would have you bear it, and so you are no losers by what we did. For the wound which is borne in God's way brings a change of heart too salutary to regret; but the hurt which is borne in the world's way brings death. You bore you hurt in God's way, and see what its results have been! It made you take the matter seriously and vindicate yourselves. How

angered you were, how apprehensive! How your longing for me awoke, yes, and your devotion and your eagerness to see justice done! At every point you have cleared yourselves of blame in this trouble. And so, although I did send you that letter, it was not the offender or his victim that most concerned me. My aim in writing was to help to make plain to you, in the sight of God, how truly you are devoted to us. That is why we have been so encouraged.
II Corinthians 7: 8-13 NEB

But our citizenship is in heaven. And we eagerly await a Savior from there, the Lord Jesus Christ, who, by the power that enables him to bring everything under his control, will transform our lowly bodies so that they will be like his glorious body. **Philippians 3: 20-21 NIV**

"Then I saw a new heaven and a new earth; for the first heaven and the first earth had passed away, and the sea was no more. And I saw the holy city, new Jerusalem, coming down out of heaven from God, prepared as a bride adorned for her husband; and I heard a great voice from the throne saying, "Behold, the dwelling of God is with men. He will dwell with them, and they shall be his people, and God himself will be with them; he will wipe away every tear from their eyes, and death shall be no more, neither shall there be mourning nor crying nor pain and more, for the former things have passed away."
Revelation 21: 1-4 RSV

COMFORT

The Lord is my shepherd, I shall not want; he makes me lie down in green pastures. He leads me beside still waters; he restores my soul. He leads me in paths of righteousness for his name's sake. Even though I walk through the valley of the shadow of death, I fear no evil; for thou art with me; thy rod and thy staff, they comfort me. Thou preparest a table before me in the presence of my enemies; thou anointest my head with oil, my cup overflows. Surely goodness and mercy shall follow me all the days of my life; and I shall dwell in the house of the Lord for ever. **Psalms 23: 1-6 RSV***

God is our refuge and strength, a very present help in trouble. Therefore we will not fear though the earth should change, though the mountains shake in the heart of the sea; though its waters roar and foam, though the mountains tremble with its tumult. There is a river whose streams make glad the city of God, the holy habitation of the Most High. God is in the midst of her, she shall not be moved; God will help her right early. The nations rage, the kingdoms totter; he utters

his voice, the earth melts. The Lord of hosts is with us; the God of Jacob is our refuge. Come, behold the works of the Lord, how he has wrought desolations in the earth. He makes wars cease to the end of the earth; he breaks the bow, and shatters the spear, he burns the chariots with fire! "Be still, and know that I am God. I am exalted among the nations, I am exalted in the earth!" The Lord of hosts is with us; the God of Jacob is our refuge.
Psalm 46: 1-11 RSV

I lift up my eyes to the hills, From whence does my help come? My help comes from the Lord, who made heaven and earth. He will not let your foot be moved, he who keeps you will not slumber. Behold, he who keeps Israel will neither slumber nor sleep. For the Lord is your keeper; the Lord is your shade on your right hand. The sun shall not smite you by day, nor the moon by night. The Lord will keep you from all evil; he will keep your life. The Lord will keep your going out and your coming in from this time forth and for evermore.
Psalm 121: 1-8 RSV

On this mountain the LORD Almighty will prepare a feast of rich food for all peoples, a banquet of aged wine—the best of meats and the finest of wines. On this mountain he will destroy the shroud that enfolds all peoples, the sheet that covers all nations; he will swallow up death forever. The Sovereign LORD will wipe away the tears from all faces; he will remove the

disgrace of his people from all the earth. The LORD has spoken. In that day they will say, "Surely this is our God; we trusted in him, and he saved us. This is the LORD, we trusted in him; let us rejoice and be glad in his salvation."
Isaiah 25: 6-9 NIV

The Spirit of the Lord God is upon me, because the Lord has anointed me to bring good tidings to the afflicted; he has sent me to bind up the brokenhearted, to proclaim liberty to the captives, and the opening of the prison to those who are bound; to proclaim the year of the Lord's favor, and the day of vengeance of our God; to comfort all who mourn; to grant to those who mourn in Zion—to give them a garland instead of ashes, the oil of gladness instead of mourning, the mantle of praise instead of a faint spirit; that they may be called oaks of righteousness, the planting of the Lord, that he may be glorified.
Isaiah 61: 1-3 RSV

At that time Jesus spoke these words: 'I thank thee, Father, Lord of heaven and earth, for hiding these things from the learned and wise, and revealing them to the simple. Yes, Father, such was thy choice. Everything is entrusted to me by my Father; and no one knows the Son but the Father, and no one knows the Father but the Son and those to whom the Son may choose to reveal him.

'Come to me, all whose work is hard, whose load is heavy; and I will give you relief. Bend your necks to my yoke, and learn from me, for I am gentle and humble-hearted; and your souls will find relief. For my yoke is good to bear, my load is light.' **Matthew 11: 25-30 NEB**

Looking at his disciples, he said: "Blessed are you who are poor, for yours is the kingdom of God. Blessed are you who hunger now, for you will be satisfied. Blessed are you who weep now, for you will laugh. Blessed are you when men hate you, when they exclude you and insult you and reject your name as evil, because of the Son of Man. Rejoice in that day and leap for joy, because great is your reward in heaven. For that is how their fathers treated the prophets." **Luke 6: 20-23 NIV**

In the same way the Spirit comes to the aid of our weakness. We do not even know how we ought to pray, but through our inarticulate groans the Spirit himself is pleading for us, and God who searches our inmost being knows what the Spirit means, because he pleads for God's own people in God's own way; and in everything, as we know, he co-operates for good with those who love God and are called according to his purpose. For God knew his own before ever they were, and also ordained that they should be shaped to the likeness of his Son, that he might be the eldest among a large family of brothers; and it is these, so for-ordained, whom he has also called. And those whom he called he has justified, and to those whom he justified he has also given his splendor.

With all this in mind, what are we to say? If God is on our side, who is against us? He did not spare his own Son, but surrendered him for us all; and with this gift how can he fail to lavish upon us all he has to give? Who will be the accuser of God's chosen ones? It is God who pronounces acquittal: then who can condemn? It is Christ—Christ who died, and, more than that, was raised from the dead—who is at God's right hand, and indeed pleads our cause. Then what can separate us from the love of Christ? Can affliction or hardship? Can persecution, hunger, nakedness, peril, or the sword? 'We are being done to death for thy sake all day long,' as Scripture says; 'we have been treated like sheep for slaughter'—and yet, in spite of all, overwhelming victory is ours through him who loved us. For I am convinced that there is nothing in death or life, in the realm of spirits or superhuman powers, in the world as it is or the world as it shall be, in the forces of the universe, in heights or depths—nothing in all creation that can separate us from the love of God in Christ Jesus our Lord.
Romans 8: 31-39 NEB+

"O death, where is your power? O death, where is your ability to destroy us?" The power of death is sin, and the strength of sin is the law. Thanks be to God, who gives us the victory through our Lord Jesus Christ!
I Corinthians 15: 55-57 HOV

Grace and peace to you from God our Father and the Lord Jesus Christ. Praise be to the God and Father of our Lord Jesus Christ, the Father of compassion and the God of all comfort, who comforts us in all our troubles, so that we can comfort those in any trouble with the comfort we ourselves have received from God. For just as the sufferings of Christ flow over into our lives, so also through Christ our comfort overflows. If we are distressed, it is for your comfort and salvation; if we are comforted, it is for your comfort, which produces in you patient endurance of the same sufferings we suffer. And our hope for you is firm, because we know that just as you share in our sufferings, so also you share in our comfort. **II Corinthians 1: 2-7 NIV**

For all these things are for your sake, so that the grace that is including more and more people may cause thanksgiving to increase to the glory of God. Therefore we do not despair, but even if our physical body is wearing away, our inner person is being renewed day by day. For our momentary, light suffering is producing for us an eternal weight of glory far beyond all comparison because we are not looking at what can be seen but at what cannot be seen. For what can be seen is temporary, but what cannot be seen is eternal.

For we know that if our earthly house, the tent we live in, is dismantled, we have a building from God, a house not built by human hands, that is eternal in the heavens. For in this earthly house we groan, because we desire to put on our heavenly dwelling, if indeed, after we have put on our heavenly house, we will not be found naked. For we groan while we are in this tent, since we are weighed down, because we do not want to be unclothed, but clothed, so that what is mortal may be swallowed up by life. **II Corinthians 4: 15- 5:4 NET**

In closing, brothers and sisters, rejoice and do what's right, encourage and trust one another, live together peacefully, and may the God of love and peace be with you. Remember to greet each other with genuine affection. All members of the fellowship send you greetings. May the grace of the Lord Jesus Christ, the love of God and the fellowship of the Holy Spirit be with you all. **II Corinthians 13: 11-13 HOV**

New Life & Healing

"If your brother sins against you, go to him and show him his fault. But do it privately, just between yourselves. If he listens to you, you have won your brother back. But if he will not listen to you, take one or two other persons with you, so that 'every accusation my be upheld by the testimony of two or more witnesses,' as the scripture says. And if he will not listen to them, then tell the whole thing to the church. Finally, if he will not listen to the church, treat him as though he were a pagan or a tax collector." **Matthew 18: 15-17 GNB**

A few days later, Jesus went back to Capernaum, and the news spread that he was at home. So many people came together that there was no room left, not even out in front of the door. Jesus was preaching the message to them when four men arrived, carrying a paralyzed man to Jesus. Because of the crowd, however, they could not get the man to him. So they made a hole in the roof right above the place where Jesus was. When they had made an opening, they let the man down, lying on his mat. Seeing how much faith they had, Jesus said to the paralyzed man, "My son, your sins are forgiven."

Some teachers of the Law who were sitting there thought to them-selves, "How does he dare talk like this? This is blasphemy! God is the only one who can forgive sins!" At once Jesus knew what they were thinking, so he said to them, "Why do you think such things? Is it easier to say to this paralyzed man, 'Your sins are forgiven,' or to say, 'Get up, pick up your mat, and walk'? I will prove to you, then, that the Son of Man has authority on earth to forgive sins." So he said to the paralyzed man, "I tell you, get up, pick up your mat, and go home!" While they all watched, the man got up, picked up his mat, and hurried away. They were all completely amazed and praised God, saying, "We have never seen anything like this!" **Mark 2: 1-12 GNB**

Jesus and his disciples arrived on the other side of Lake Galilee, in the territory of Gerasa. As soon as Jesus got out of the boat, he was met by a man who came out of the burial caves there. This man had an evil spirit in him and lived among the tombs. Nobody could keep him tied with chains any more; many times his feet and his hands had been tied, but every time he broke the chains and smashed the irons on his feet. He was too strong for anyone to control him. Day and night he wandered among the tombs and through the hills, screaming and cutting himself with stones.

He was some distance away when he saw Jesus; so he ran, fell on his knees before him, and screamed in a loud voice, "Jesus, Son of the Most High God! What do you want with me? For God's sake, I beg you, don't punish me!" (He said this because Jesus was saying, "Evil spirit, come out of this man!") So Jesus asked him, "What is your name?" The man answered, "My name is 'Mob'—there are so many of us!" And he kept begging Jesus not to send the evil spirits out of that region. There was a large herd of pigs near by, feeding on a hillside. So the spirits begged Jesus, "Send us to the pigs, and let us go into them." He let them go, and the evil spirits went out of the man and entered the pigs. The whole herd—about two thousand pigs in all—rushed down the side of the cliff into the lake and was drowned.

The men who had been taking care of the pigs ran away and spread the news in the town and among the farms. People went out to see what had happened, and when they came to Jesus, they saw the man who used to have the mob of demons in him. He was sitting there, clothed and in his right mind; and they were all afraid. Those who had seen it told the people what had happened to the man with demons, and about the pigs. So they asked Jesus to leave their territory. As Jesus was getting into the boat, the man who had had the demons begged him, "Let me go with you!" But Jesus would not let him. Instead, he told him, "Go back home to your family and tell them how much the Lord has done for you and how kind he has been to you." So the man left and went all through the Ten Towns, telling what Jesus had done for him. And all who heard it were amazed. **Mark 5: 1-20 GNB**

A man suffering from a dreaded skin disease came to Jesus, knelt down, and begged him for help. "If you want to," he said, "you can make me clean." Jesus was filled with pity, and reached out and touched him. "I do want to," he answered. "Be clean!" At once the disease left the man, and he was clean. **Mark 1: 40-42 GNB**

At that very time Jesus cured many who had diseases, sicknesses and evil spirits, and gave sight to many who were blind. So he replied to the messengers, "Go back and report to John what you have seen and heard: The blind receive sight, the lame walk, those who have leprosy are cured, the deaf hear, the dead are raised, and the good news is preached to the poor. Blessed is the man who does not fall away on account of me." **Luke 7: 21-23 NIV**

There was one of the Pharisees named Nicodemus, a member of the Jewish Council, who came to Jesus by night. 'Rabbi,' he said, 'we know that you are a teacher sent by God; no one could perform these sign of yours unless God were with him.' Jesus answered, 'In truth, in very truth I tell you, unless a man has been born over again he cannot see the kingdom of God.' 'But how is it possible', said Nicodemus, 'for a man to be born when he is old? Can he enter his mother's womb a second time and be born?' Jesus answered, 'In truth I tell you, no one can enter the kingdom of God without being born from water and spirit. Flesh can give birth only to flesh; it is spirit that gives birth to spirit. You ought not to be astonished, then, when I tell you that you must be born over again. The wind blows where it wills; you hear the sound of it, but you do not know where it comes from, or where it is going. So with everyone who is born from spirit.'

Nicodemus replied, 'How is this possible?' 'What!' said Jesus, 'Is this famous teacher of Israel ignorant of such things? In very truth I tell you, we speak of what we know, and testify to what we have seen, and yet you all reject our testimony. If you disbelieve me when I talk to you about things on earth, how are you to believe if I should talk about the things of heaven? 'No one ever went up into heaven except the one who came down from heaven, the Son of Man whose home is in heaven. This Son of Man must be lifted up as the serpent was lifted up by Moses in the wilderness, so that everyone who has faith in him may in him possess eternal life.

'God loved the world so much that he gave his only Son, that everyone who has faith in him may not die but have eternal life. It was not to judge the world that God sent his Son into the world, but that through him the world might be saved. **John 3: 1-17 NEB+**

The disciples had gone away to the town to buy food. Meanwhile a Samaritan woman came to draw water. Jesus said to her, 'Give me a drink.' The Samaritan woman said, 'What! You, a Jew, ask a drink of me, a Samaritan woman?' (Jews and Samaritans, it should be noted, do not use vessels in common.) Jesus answered her, 'If only you knew what God gives, and who it is that is asking you for a drink, you would have asked him and he would have given you living water.' 'Sir,' the woman said, 'you have no bucket and this well is deep. How can you give me "living water"? Are you a greater man than Jacob our ancestor, who gave us the well, and drank from it himself, he and his sons, and his cattle too?' Jesus said, 'Everyone who drinks this water will be thirsty again, but whoever drinks the water that I shall give him will never suffer thirst any more. The water that I shall give him will be an inner spring always welling up for eternal life.' **John 4: 7-14 NEB**

Now as Jesus was passing by, he saw a man who had been blind from birth. His disciples asked him, "Rabbi, who committed the sin that caused him to be born blind, this man or his parents?" Jesus answered, "Neither this man nor his parents sinned, but he was born blind so that the acts of God may be revealed through what happens to him. We must perform the deeds of the one who sent me as long as it is daytime. Night is coming when no one can work. As long as I am in the world, I am the light of the world." Having said this, he spat on the ground and made some mud with the saliva. He smeared the mud on the blind man's eyes and said to him, "Go wash in the pool of Siloam" (which is translated "sent"). o the blind man went away and washed, and came back seeing. Then the neighbors and the people who had seen him previously as a beggar began saying, "Is this not the man who used to sit and beg?" Some people said, "This is the man!" while others said, "No, but he looks like him." The man himself kept insisting, "I am the one!" So they asked him, "How then were you made to see?" He replied, "The man called Jesus made mud, smeared it on my eyes and told me, 'Go to Siloam and wash.' So I went and washed, and was able to see." **John 9: 1-11 NET**

Truly, truly, I say to you, he who does not enter the sheepfold by the door but climbs in by another way, that man is a thief and a robber; but he who enters by the door is the shepherd of the sheep. To him the gatekeeper opens; the sheep hear his voice, and he calls his own sheep by name and leads them out. When he has brought out all his own, he goes before them, and the sheep follow him, for they know his voice. A stranger they will not follow, but they will flee from him, for they do not know the voice of strangers." This figure Jesus used with them, but they did not understand what he was saying to them.

So Jesus again said to them, "Truly, truly, I say to you, I am the door of the sheep. All who came before me are thieves and robbers; but the sheep did not heed them.

I am the door; if any one enters by me, he will be saved, and will go in and out and find pasture. The thief comes only to steal and kill and destroy; I came that they may have life, and have it abundantly. I am the good shepherd. The good shepherd lays down his life for the sheep. He who is a hireling and not a shepherd, whose own the sheep are not, sees the wolf coming and leaves the sheep and flees; and the wolf snatches them and scatters them. He flees because he is a hireling and cares nothing for the sheep. I am the good shepherd; I know my own know me, and my own know me, as the Father knows me and I know the Father; and I lay down my life for the sheep. And I have other sheep, that are not of this fold; I must bring them also, and they will heed my voice. So there shall be one flock, and one shepherd. For this reason the Father loves me, because I lay down my life, that I may take it again. No one takes it from me, but I lay down of my own accord. I have power to lay it down, and I have power to take it again; this charge I have received from my Father."
John 10: 1-18 RSV

Now a certain man named Lazarus was sick. He was from Bethany, the village where Mary and her sister Martha lived. (Now it was Mary who anointed the Lord with perfumed oil and wiped his feet dry with her hair, whose brother Lazarus was sick.)

So the sisters sent a message to Jesus, "Lord, look, the one you love is sick." When Jesus heard this, he said,

"This sickness will not lead to death, but to God's glory, so that the Son of God may be glorified through it." (Now Jesus loved Martha and her sister and Lazarus.)

So when he heard that Lazarus was sick, he remained in the place where he was for two more days. Then after this, he said to his disciples, "Let us go to Judea again." The disciples replied, "Rabbi, the Jewish leaders were just now trying to stone you to death! Are you going there again?" Jesus replied, "Are there not twelve hours in a day? If anyone walks around in the daytime, he does not stumble, because he sees the light of this world. But if anyone walks around at night, he stumbles, because the light is not in him."

After he said this, he added, "Our friend Lazarus has fallen asleep. But I am going there to awaken him." Then the disciples replied, "Lord, if he has fallen asleep, he will recover." (Now Jesus had been talking about his death, but they thought he had been talking about real sleep.) Then Jesus told them plainly, "Lazarus has died, and I am glad for your sake that I was not there, so that you may believe. But let us go to him." So Thomas (called Didymus) said to his fellow disciples, "Let us go too, so that we may die with him."

When Jesus arrived, he found that Lazarus had been in the tomb four days already. (Now Bethany was less than two miles from Jerusalem, so many of the Jewish people of the region had come to Martha and Mary to console them over the loss of their brother.) So when Martha heard that Jesus was coming, she went out to meet him, but Mary was sitting in the house. Martha said to Jesus, "Lord, if you had been here, my brother would not have died. But even now I know that whatever you ask from God, God will grant you."

Jesus replied, "Your brother will come back to life again." Martha said, "I know that he will come back to life again in the resurrection at the last day." Jesus said to her, "I am the resurrection and the life. The one who believes in me will live even if he dies, and the one who lives and believes in me will never die. Do you believe this?" She replied, "Yes, Lord, I believe that you are the Christ, the Son of God who comes into the world."

And when she had said this, Martha went and called her sister Mary, saying privately, "The Teacher is here and is asking for you." So when Mary heard this, she got up quickly and went to him. (Now Jesus had not yet entered the village, but was still in the place where Martha had come out to meet him.) Then the people who were with Mary in the house consoling her saw her get up quickly and go out. They followed her, because they thought she was going to the tomb to weep there.

Now when Mary came to the place where Jesus was and saw him, she fell at his feet and said to him, "Lord, if you had been here, my brother would not have died." When Jesus saw her weeping, and the people who had come with her weeping, he was intensely moved in spirit and greatly distressed. He asked, "Where have you laid him?" They replied, "Lord, come and see." Jesus wept. Thus the people who had come to mourn said, "Look how much he loved him!" But some of them said, "This is the man who caused the blind man to see! Couldn't he have done something to keep Lazarus from dying?"

Jesus, intensely moved again, came to the tomb. (Now it was a cave, and a stone was placed across it.) Jesus said, "Take away the stone." Martha, the sister of the deceased, replied, "Lord, by this time the body will have a bad smell, because he has been buried four days." Jesus responded, "Didn't I tell you that if you believe, you would see the glory of God?" So they took away the stone. Jesus looked upward and said, "Father, I thank you that you have listened to me. I knew that you always listen to me, but I said this for the sake of the crowd standing around here, that they may believe that you sent me." When he had said this, he shouted in a loud voice, "Lazarus, come out!" The one who had died came out, his feet and hands tied up with strips of cloth, and a cloth wrapped around his face. Jesus said to them, "Unwrap him and let him go." **John 11: 1-44 NET**

One day Peter and John went to the Temple at three o'clock in the afternoon, the hour for prayer. There at the Beautiful Gate, as it was called, was a man who had been lame all his life. Every day he was carried to the gate to beg for money from the people who were going into the Temple. When he saw Peter and John going in, he begged them to give him something. They looked straight at him, and Peter said, "Look at us!" So he looked at them, expecting to get something from them. But Peter said to him, "I have no money at all, but I give you what I have: in the name of Jesus Christ of Nazareth I order you to get up and walk!" Then he took him by his right hand and helped him up. At once the man's feet and ankles became strong; he jumped up, stood on his feet, and started walking around. Then he went into the Temple with them, walking and jumping and praising God. The people there saw him walking and praising God, and when they recognized him as the beggar who had sat at the Beautiful Gate, they were all surprised and amazed at what had happened to him.

As the man held on to Peter and John in Solomon's Porch, as it was called, the people were amazed and ran to them. When Peter saw the people, he said to them, "Fellow Israelites, why are you surprised at this, and why do you stare at us? Do you think that it was by means of our own power or godliness that we made this man walk? The God of Abraham, Isaac, and Jacob, the God of our ancestors, has given divine glory to his Servant Jesus. But you handed him over to the authorities, and you rejected him in Pilate's presence, even after Pilate had decided to set him free. He was holy and good, but you rejected him, and instead you asked Pilate to do you the favor of turning loose a murderer. You killed the one who leads to life, but God raised him from death—and we are witnesses to this. It was the power of his name that gave strength to this lame man. What you see and know was done by faith in his name; it was faith in Jesus that has made him well, as you can all see. **Acts 3: 1-16 GNB**

In Lystra sat a man who could not use his feet, lame from birth, who had never walked. This man was listening to Paul as he was speaking. When Paul stared intently at him and saw he had faith to be healed, he said with a loud voice, "Stand upright on your feet." And the man leaped up and began walking. So when the crowds saw what Paul had done, they shouted in the Lycaonian language, "The gods have come down to us in human form!" They began to call Barnabas Zeus and Paul Hermes, because he was the chief speaker. The priest of the temple of Zeus, located just outside the city, brought bulls and garlands to the city gates; he and the crowds wanted to offer sacrifices to them. But when the apostles Barnabas and Paul heard about it, they tore their clothes and rushed out into the crowd, shouting, "Men, why are you doing these things? We too are men, with human natures just like you! We are proclaiming the good news to you, so that you should turn from these worthless things to the living God, who made the heaven, the earth, the sea, and everything that is in them. In past generations he allowed all the nations to go their own ways, yet he did not leave himself without a witness by doing good, by giving you rain from heaven and fruitful seasons, satisfying you with food and your hearts with joy." Even by saying these things, they scarcely persuaded the crowds not to offer sacrifice to them. **Acts 14: 8-18 NET**

The conclusion of the matter is this: there is no condemnation for those who are united with Christ Jesus, because in Christ Jesus the life-giving law of the Spirit has set you free from the law of sin and death. What the law could never do, because our lower nature robbed it of all potency, God has done: by sending his own Son in a form like that of our own sinful nature, and as a sacrifice for sin, he has passed judgment against sin within that very nature, so that the commandment of the law may find fulfillment in us, whose conduct, no longer under the control of our lower nature, is directed by the Spirit.

Those who live on the level of our lower nature have their outlook formed by it, and that spells death; but those who live on the level of the spirit have the spiritual outlook, and that is life and peace. For the outlook of the lower nature is enmity with God; it is not subject to the law of God; indeed it cannot be: those who live on such a level cannot possibly please God.

But that is not how you live. You are on the spiritual level, if only God's Spirit dwells within you; and if a man does not possess the Spirit of Christ, he is no Christian. But if Christ is dwelling within you, then although the body is a dead thing because you sinned, yet the spirit is life itself because you have been justified. Moreover, if the Spirit of him who raised Jesus from the dead dwells within you, then the God who raised Christ Jesus from the dead will also give new life to your mortal bodies through his indwelling Spirit. **Romans 8: 1-13 NEB**

THANKFULNESS

Now on his way to Jerusalem, Jesus traveled along the border between Samaria and Galilee. As he was going into a village, ten men who had leprosy met him. They stood at a distance and called out in a loud voice, "Jesus, Master, have pity on us!" When he saw them, he said, "Go, show yourselves to the priests." And as they went, they were cleansed. One of them, when he saw he was healed, came back, praising God in a loud voice. He threw himself at Jesus' feet and thanked him—and he was a Samaritan. Jesus asked, "Were not all ten cleansed? Where are the other nine? Was no one found to return and give praise to God except this foreigner?" Then he said to him, "Rise and go; your faith has made you well." **Luke 17: 11-19 NIV**

I always thank my God for you because of the grace of God that was given to you in Christ Jesus. For you were made rich in every way in him, in all your speech and in every kind of knowledge –just as the testimony about Christ has been confirmed among you –so that you do not lack any spiritual gift as you wait for the revelation

of our Lord Jesus Christ. He will also strengthen you to the end, so that you will be blameless on the day of our Lord Jesus Christ. God is faithful, by whom you were called into fellowship with his son, Jesus Christ our Lord.
I Corinthians 1: 4-9 NET

But thanks be to God, who continually leads us about, captives in Christ's triumphal procession, and everywhere uses us to reveal and spread abroad the fragrance of the knowledge of himself! We are indeed the incense offered by Christ to God, both for those who are the way to salvation, and for those who on the way to perdition: to the latter it is a deadly fume that kills, to the former a vital fragrance that brings life. Who is equal to such a calling? At least we do not go hawking the word of God about, as so many do; when we declare the word we do it in sincerity, as from God and in God's sight, as members of Christ. **II Corinthians 2: 14-17 NEB**

Each one of you should give just as he has decided in his heart, not reluctantly or under compulsion, because God loves a cheerful giver. And God is able to make all grace overflow to you so that because you have enough of everything in every way at all times, you will overflow in every good work. Just as it is written, "He has scattered widely, he has given to the poor; his righteousness remains forever." Now God who provides seed for the sower and bread for food will provide and multiply your supply of seed and will cause the harvest of your righteousness to grow. You will be enriched in every way so that you may be generous on every occasion, which is producing through us thanksgiving to God, because the service of this ministry is not only providing for the needs of the saints but is also overflowing with many thanks to God. Through the evidence of this service they will glorify God because of your obedience to your confession in the gospel of Christ and the generosity of your sharing with them and with everyone. And in their prayers on your behalf they long for you because of the extraordinary grace God has shown to you. Thanks be to God for his indescribable gift! **II Corinthians 9: 7-15 NET~**

Because of all this, now that I have heard of the faith you have in the Lord Jesus and of the love you bear towards all God's people, I never cease to give thanks for you when I mention you in my prayers. I pray that the God of our Lord Jesus Christ, the all-glorious Father, may give you the spiritual powers of wisdom and vision, by which there comes the knowledge of him. I pray that your inward eyes may be illuminated, so that you may know what is the hope to which he calls you, what the wealth and glory of the share he offers you among his people in their heritage, and how vast the resources of his power open to us who trust in him. They are measured by his strength and the might which he exerted in Christ when he raised him from the dead, when he enthroned him at his right hand in the heavenly realms, far above all government and authority, all power and dominion, and any title of sovereignty that can be named, not only in this age but in the age to come. He put everything in subjection beneath his feet, and appointed him as supreme head to the church, which is his body and as such holds within it the fullness of him who himself receives the entire fullness of God. **Ephesians 1: 15-23 NEB**

I thank my God for you every time I think of you; and every time I pray for you all, I pray with joy because of the way in which you have helped me in the work of the gospel from the very first day until now. And so I am sure that God, who began this good work in you, will carry it on until it is finished on the Day of Christ Jesus. You are always in my heart! And so it is only right for me to feel as I do about you. For you have all shared with me in this privilege that God has given me, both now that I am in prison and also while I was free to defend the gospel and establish it firmly. God is my witness that I tell the truth when I say that my deep feeling for you all comes from the heart of Christ Jesus himself.

I pray that your love will keep on growing more and more, together with true knowledge and perfect judgment, so that you will be able to choose what is best. Then you will be free from all impurity and blame on the Day of Christ. Your lives will be filled with the truly good qualities which only Jesus Christ can produce, for the glory and praise of God. **Philippians 1:3-11 GNB**

Rejoice in the Lord always. I will say it again: Rejoice! Let your gentleness be evident to all. The Lord is near. Do not be anxious about anything, but in everything, by prayer and petition, with thanksgiving, present your requests to God. And the peace of God, which transcends all understanding, will guard your hearts and your minds in Christ Jesus.

Finally, brothers, whatever is true, whatever is noble, whatever is right, whatever is pure, whatever is lovely, whatever is admirable—if anything is excellent or praiseworthy—think about such things. Whatever you have learned or received or heard from me, or seen in me—put it into practice. And the God of peace will be with you. **Philippians 4: 4-9 NIV**

Since you have accepted Christ Jesus as Lord, live in union with him. Keep your roots deep in him, build your lives on him, and become stronger in your faith, as you were taught. And be filled with thanksgiving. **Colossians 2: 6-7 GNB**

FAITH

Then he made the disciples embark and go on ahead to the other side, while he sent the people away; after doing that, he went up the hill-side to pray alone. It grew late, and he was there by himself. The boat was already some furlongs from the shore, battling with a head-wind and a rough sea. Between three and six in the morning he came to them, walking over the lake. When the disciples saw him walking on the lake they were so shaken that they cried out in terror: 'It is a ghost!' But at once he spoke to them: 'Take heart! It is I; do not be afraid.'

Peter called to him: 'Lord, if it is you, tell me to come to you over the water.' 'Come', said Jesus. Peter stepped down from the boat, and walked over the water toward Jesus. But when he saw the strength of the gale he was seized with fear; and beginning to sink, he cried, 'Save me, Lord.' Jesus at once reached out and caught hold of him, and said, 'Why did you hesitate? How little faith you have!' They then climbed into the boat; and the wind dropped. And the men in the boat fell at his feet, exclaiming, 'Truly you are the Son of God.' **Matthew 14: 22-33 NEB**

"If anyone should cause one of these little ones to lose his faith in me, it would be better for that person to have large millstone tied around his neck and be drowned in the deep sea. How terrible for the world that there are things that make people lose their faith! Such things will always happen—but how terrible for the one who causes them!

If your hand or your foot makes you lose your faith, cut it off and throw it away! It is better for you to enter life without a hand or a foot than to keep both hands and both feet and be thrown into the eternal fire. And if your eye makes you lose your faith, take it out and throw it away! It is better for you to enter life with only one eye than to keep both eyes and be thrown into the fire of hell." **Matthew 18: 6-9 GNB**

When Jesus had finished saying all this in the hearing of the people, he entered Capernaum. There a centurion's servant, whom his master valued highly, was sick and about to die. The centurion heard of Jesus and sent some elders of the Jews to him, asking him to come and heal his servant. When they came to Jesus, they pleaded earnestly with him, "This man deserves to have you do this, because he loves our nation and has built our synagogue." So Jesus went with them.

He was not far from the house when the centurion sent friends to say to him: "Lord, don't trouble yourself, for I do not deserve to have you come under my roof. That is why I did not even consider myself worthy to come to you. But say the word, and my servant will be healed. For I myself am a man under authority, with soldiers under me. I tell this one, 'Go,' and he goes; and that one, 'Come,' and he comes. I say to my servant, 'Do this,' and he does it."

When Jesus heard this, he was amazed at him, and turning to the crowd following him, he said, "I tell you, I have not found such great faith even in Israel." Then the men who had been sent returned to the house and found the servant well. **Luke 7: 1-10 NIV**

He spoke the them in a parable to show that they should keep on praying and never lose heart: 'There was once a judge who cared nothing for God or man, and in the same town there was a widow who constantly came before him demanding justice against her opponent. For a long time he refused; but in the end he said to himself, "True, I care nothing for God or man; but this widow is so great a nuisance that I will see her righted before she wears me out with her persistence."' The Lord said, 'You hear what the unjust judge says; and will not God vindicate his chosen, who cry out to him day and night, while he listens patiently to them? I tell you, he will vindicate them soon enough. But when

the Son of Man comes, will he find faith on earth?'
Luke 18: 1-8 NEB

First, I am thankful to my God through Jesus Christ for all of you, since your faith is acknowledged around the world. God, whom I serve by preaching the gospel of his Son, is my witness that I continually remember you and prayerfully ask that I might be able to come and see you. I deeply desire to be with you, God willing, so that I can pass on some spiritual gifts to strengthen you. What I am trying to say is that hopefully both you and I will be comforted as we have our faith strengthened.
Romans 1: 8-12 HOV

What, then, are we to say about Abraham, our ancestor in the natural line? If Abraham was justified by anything he had done, then he has a ground for pride. But he has no such ground before God; for what does Scripture say? 'Abraham put his faith in God, and that faith was counted to him as righteousness.' Now if a man does a piece of work, his wages are not 'counted' as a favor; they are paid as debt. But if without any work to his credit he simply puts his faith in him who acquits the guilty, then his faith is indeed 'counted as righteousness'. In the same sense David speaks of the happiness of the man whom God 'counts' as just, apart from any specific acts of justice: 'Happy are they', he says, 'whose lawless deeds are forgiven, whose sins are buried away; happy is the man whose sins the Lord does not count against him.' Is this happiness confined to the circumcised, or is it for the uncircumcised also? Consider: we say, 'Abraham's faith was counted as righteousness'; in what circumstances was it so counted? Was he circumcised at the time or not? He was not yet circumcised, but uncircumcised; and he later received the symbolic rite of circumcision as the hallmark of the righteousness which faith had given him when he was still uncircumcised. Consequently, he is the father of all who have faith when uncircumcised, so that righteousness is 'counted' to them; and at the same time he is the father of such of the circumcised as do not rely upon their circumcision alone, but also walk in the footprints of the faith which our father Abraham had while he was yet uncircumcised.

For it was not through law that Abraham, or his posterity, was given the promise that the world should be his inheritance, but through the righteousness that came from faith. For if those who hold by the law, and they alone, are heirs, then faith is empty and the promise goes for nothing, because law can bring on retribution; but where there is no law there can be no breach of law. The promise was made on the ground of faith, in order that it might be a matter of sheer grace, and that it might be valid for all Abraham's posterity, not only for those who hold by the law, but for those also who have the faith of Abraham. For he is the father of us all, as Scripture says: 'I have appointed you to be father of many nations.' This promise, then, was valid before God, the God in whom he put his faith, the God who makes the dead live and summons things that are not yet in existence as if they already were. When hope seemed hopeless, his faith was such that he became 'father of many nations', in agreement with the words which had been spoken to him: 'Thus shall your posterity be.' Without any weakening of faith he contemplated his own body, as good as dead (for he was about a hundred years old), and the deadness of Sarah's womb, and never doubted God's promise, but, strong in faith, gave honor to God, in the firm conviction of his power to do what he had promised. And that is why Abraham's faith was 'counted to him as righteousness'.

Those words were written, not for Abraham's sake alone, but for our sake too: it is to be 'counted' in the same way to us who have faith in the God who raised Jesus our Lord from the dead; for he was delivered to death for our misdeeds, and raised to life to justify us.
Romans 4: 1-25 NEB

If you confess that Jesus is Lord and believe that God raised him from death, you will be saved. For it is by our faith that we are put right with God; it is by our confession that we are saved. The scripture says, "Whoever believes in him will not be disappointed." This includes everyone, because there is no difference between Jews and Gentiles; God is the same Lord of all and richly blesses all who call to him. As the scripture says, "Everyone who calls out to the Lord for help will be saved."

But how can they call to him for help if they have not believed? And how can they believe if they have not heard the message? And how can they hear if the message is not proclaimed? And how can the message be proclaimed if the messengers are not sent out? As the scripture says, "How wonderful is the coming of messengers who bring good news!" But not all have accepted the Good News. Isaiah himself said, "Lord, who believed our message?" So then, faith comes from hearing the message, and the message comes through preaching Christ. **Romans 10: 9-17 GNB**

It is written: "I believed; therefore I have spoken." With that same spirit of faith we also believe and therefore speak, because we know that the one who raised the Lord Jesus from the dead will also raise us with Jesus and present us with you in his presence. All this is for your benefit, so that the grace that is reaching more and more people may cause thanksgiving to overflow to the glory of God. **II Corinthians 4: 13-15 NIV**

We ourselves are Jews by birth, not Gentiles and sinners. But we know that no man is ever justified by doing what the law demands, but only through faith in Christ Jesus; so we too have put our faith in Jesus Christ, in order that we might be justified through this faith, and not through deeds dictated by law; for by such deeds, Scripture says, no mortal man shall be justified.

If now, in seeking to be justified in Christ, we ourselves

no less than the Gentiles turn out to be sinners against the law, does that mean that Christ is an abettor of sin? No, never! No, if I start building up again a system which I have pulled down, then it is that I show myself up as a transgressor of the law. For through the law I died to law—to live for God. I have been crucified with Christ: the life I now live is not my life, but the life which Christ lives in me; and my present bodily life is lived by faith in the Son of God, who loved me and sacrificed himself for me. I will not nullify the grace of God; if righteousness comes by law, then Christ died for nothing.
Galatians 2: 15-21 NEB~

Now before faith came we were held in custody under the law, being kept as prisoners until the coming faith would be revealed. Thus the law had become our guardian until Christ, so that we could be declared righteous by faith. But now that faith has come, we are no longer under a guardian. For in Christ Jesus you are all sons of God through faith. For all of you who were baptized into Christ have clothed yourselves with Christ. There is neither Jew nor Greek, there is neither slave nor free, there is neither male nor female – for all of you are one in Christ Jesus. And if you belong to Christ, then you are Abraham's descendants, heirs according to the promise.

Now I mean that the heir, as long as he is a minor, is no different from a slave, though he is the owner of

everything. But he is under guardians and managers until the date set by his father. So also we, when we were minors, were enslaved under the basic forces of the world. But when the appropriate time had come, God sent out his Son, born of a woman, born under the law, to redeem those who were under the law, so that we may be adopted as sons with full rights. And because you are sons, God sent the Spirit of his Son into our hearts, who calls "Abba! Father!" So you are no longer a slave but a son, and if you are a son, then you are also an heir through God.
Galatians 3: 23- 4: 7 NET

As far as a person can be righteous by obeying the commands of the Law, I was without fault. But all those things that I might count as profit I now reckon as loss for Christ's sake. Not only those things; I reckon everything as complete loss for the sake of what is so much more valuable, the knowledge of Christ Jesus my Lord. For his sake I have thrown everything away; I consider it all as mere garbage, so that I may gain Christ and be completely united with him. I no longer have a righteousness of my own, the kind that is gained by obeying the Law. I now have the righteousness that is given through faith in Christ, the righteousness that comes from God and is based on faith. All I want is to know Christ and to experience the power of his resurrection, to share in his sufferings and become like him in his death, in the hope that I myself will be raised from death to life.
Philippians 3: 6-11 GNB+

Now faith is being sure of what we hope for and certain of what we do not see. This is what the ancients were commended for. By faith we understand that the universe was formed at God's command, so that what is seen was not made out of what was visible. **Hebrews 11: 1-3 NIV**

By faith Abraham obeyed when he was called to go out to a place which he was to receive as an inheritance; and he went out, not knowing where he was to go. By faith he sojourned in the land of promise, as in a foreign land, living in tents with Isaac and Jacob, heirs with him of the same promise. For he looked forward to the city which has foundations, whose builder and maker is God. By faith Sarah herself received power to conceive, even when she was past the age, since she considered him faithful who had promised. Therefore from one man, and him as good as dead, were born descendants as many as the stars of heaven and as the innumerable grains of sand by the seashore. **Hebrews 11: 8-12 RSV**

By faith Abraham, when he was tested, offered up Isaac, and he who had received the promises was ready to offer up his only son, of whom it was said, "Through Isaac shall your descendants be named." He considered that God was able to raise men even from the dead; hence, figuratively speaking, he did receive him back. By faith Isaac invoked future blessings on Jacob and Esau. By faith Jacob, when dying, blessed each of the sons of Joseph, bowing in worship over the head of his staff. By faith Joseph, at the end of his life, made mention of the exodus of the Israelites and gave directions concerning his burial. **Hebrews 11: 17-22 RSV**

And all these, though well attested by their faith, did not receive what was promised, since God had foreseen something better for us, that apart from us they should not be made perfect.

Therefore, since we are surrounded by so great a cloud of witnesses, let us also lay aside every weight, and sin which clings to closely, and let us run with perseverance the race that is set before us, looking to Jesus the pioneer and perfecter of our faith, who for the joy that was set before him endured the cross, despising the shame, and is seated at the right hand of the throne of God.
Hebrews 11: 39- 12: 2 RSV~

My brothers, what good is it for someone to say that he has faith if his actions do not prove it? Can that faith save him? Suppose there are brothers or sisters who need clothes and don't have enough to eat. What good is there in your saying to them, "God bless you! Keep warm and eat well!"—if you don't give them the necessities of life? So it is with faith: if it is alone and includes no actions, then it is dead.

But someone will say, "One person has faith, another has actions." My answer is, "Show me how anyone can have faith without actions. I will show you my faith by my actions." Do you believe that there is only one God? Good! The demons also believe—and tremble with fear. You fool! Do you want to be shown that faith without actions is useless? How was our ancestor Abraham put right with God? It was through his actions, when he offered his son Isaac on the altar. Can't you see? His faith and his actions worked together; his faith was made perfect through his actions. And the scripture came true that said, "Abraham believed God, and because of his faith God accepted him as righteous." And so Abraham was called God's friend. You see, then, that it is by his actions that a person is put right with God, and not by his faith alone.

It was the same with the prostitute Rahab. She was put right with God through her actions, by welcoming the Israelite spies and helping them to escape by a different road. So then, as the body without the spirit is dead, also faith without actions is dead. **James 2: 14-26 GNB**

Be alert, be on watch! Your enemy, the Devil, roams around like a roaring lion, looking for someone to devour. Be firm in your faith and resist him, because you know that your fellow believers in all the world are going through the same kind of sufferings. But after you have suffered for a little while, the God of all grace, who calls you to share his eternal glory in union with Christ, will himself perfect you and give you firmness, strength, and a sure foundation. To him be the power forever! Amen. **I Peter 5: 8-11 GNB**

Jesus Christ is the one who came with the water of his baptism and the blood of his death. He came not only with the water, but with both the water and the blood. And the Spirit himself testifies that this is true, because the Spirit is truth. There are three witnesses: the Spirit, the water, and the blood; and all three give the same testimony. We believe man's testimony; but God's testimony is much stronger, and he has given this testimony about his Son. So whoever believes in the Son of God has this testimony in his own heart; but whoever does not believe God, has made a liar out of him, because he has not believed what God has said about his Son. The testimony is this: God has given us eternal life, and this life has its source in his Son. Whoever has the Son has this life; whoever does not have the Son of God does not have life. **I John 5: 6-12 GNB**

Hope

Then God said to Noah and to his sons with him, "Behold, I establish my covenant with you and your descendants after you, and with every living creature that is with you, the birds, the cattle, and every beast of the earth with you, as many as came out of the ark. I establish my covenant with you, that never again shall all flesh be cut off by the waters of a flood, and never again shall there be a flood to destroy the earth."

And God said, "This is the sign of the covenant which I make between me and you and every living creature that is with you, for all future generations: I set my bow in the cloud, and it shall be a sign of the covenant between me and the earth. When I bring clouds over the earth and the bow is seen in the clouds, I will remember my covenant which is between me and you and every living creature of all flesh; and the waters shall never again become a flood to destroy all flesh. When the bow is in the clouds, I will look upon it and remember the everlasting covenant between God and every living creature of all flesh that is upon the earth." God said to Noah, "This is the sign of the covenant which I have established between me and all flesh that is upon the earth." **Genesis 9: 8-17 RSV**

Out of the depths I cry to thee, O Lord! Lord hear my voice! Let thy ears be attentive to the voice of my supplications! If thou, O Lord, shouldst mark iniquities, Lord, who could stand? But there is forgiveness with thee, that thou mayest be feared. I wait for the Lord, my soul waits, and in his word I hope; my soul waits for the Lord more than watchmen for the morning, more than watchmen for the morning. O Israel, hope in the Lord! For with the Lord there is steadfast love, and with him is plenteous redemption. And he will redeem Israel

from all his iniquities. **Psalm 130: 1-8 RSV**

Blessed is he whose help is the God of Jacob, whose hope is in the LORD his God, the Maker of heaven and earth, the sea, and everything in them—the LORD, who remains faithful forever. He upholds the cause of the oppressed and gives food to the hungry.

The LORD sets prisoners free, the LORD gives sight to the blind, the LORD lifts up those who are bowed down, the LORD loves the righteous. The LORD watches over the alien and sustains the fatherless and the widow, but he frustrates the ways of the wicked. **Psalms 146: 5-9 NIV**

Therefore, since we have been declared righteous by faith, we have peace with God through our Lord Jesus Christ, through whom we have also obtained access by faith into this grace in which we stand, and we rejoice in the hope of God's glory. Not only this, but we also rejoice in sufferings, knowing that suffering produces endurance, and endurance, character, and character, hope. And hope does not disappoint, because the love of God has been poured out in our hearts through the Holy Spirit who was given to us. **Romans 5: 1-5 NET+**

For I reckon that the sufferings we now endure bear no comparison with the splendor, as yet unrevealed, which is in store for us. For the created universe waits with eager expectation for God's sons to be revealed. It was made the victim of frustration, not by its own choice, but because of him who made it so; yet always there was hope, because the universe itself is to be freed from the shackles of mortality and enter upon the liberty and splendor of the children of God. Up to the present, we know, the whole created universe groans it all its parts as if in the pangs of childbirth. Not only so, but even we, to whom the Spirit is given as firstfruits of the harvest to come, are groaning inwardly while we wait for God to make us his sons and set our whole body free. For we have been saved, though only in hope. Now to see is no longer to hope: why should a man endure and wait for what he already sees? But it we hope for something we do not yet see, then, in waiting for it, we show our endurance. **Romans 8: 18-25 NEB+**

And may the God of hope fill you with all joy and peace by your faith in him, until, by the power of the Holy Spirit, you overflow with hope. **Romans 15: 13 NEB**

In saying this, we should like you to know, dear friends, how serious was the trouble that came upon us in the province of Asia. The burden of it was far too heavy for us to bear, so heavy that we even despaired of life. Indeed, we felt in our hearts that we had received a death-sentence. This was meant to teach us not to place reliance on ourselves, but on God who raises the dead. From such mortal peril God delivered us; and he will deliver us again, he on whom our hope is fixed. Yes, he will continue to deliver us, if you will co-operate by praying for us. Then, with so many people praying for our deliverance, there will be many to give thanks on our behalf for the gracious favor God has shown towards us.
II Corinthians 1: 8-11 NEB

When the true message, the Good News, first came to you, you heard about the hope it offers. So your faith and love are based on what you hope for, which is kept safe for you in heaven. The Gospel keeps bringing blessings and is spreading throughout the world, just as it has among you ever since the day you first heard about the grace of God and came to know it as it really is.
Colossians 1: 3-6 GNB

For the grace of God has dawned upon the world with healing for all mankind; and by it we are disciplined

to renounce godless ways and worldly desires, and to live a life of temperance, honesty, and godliness in the present age, looking forward to the happy fulfillment of our hopes when the splendor of our great God and Savior Christ Jesus will appear. He it is who sacrificed himself for us, to set us free from all wickedness and to make us a pure people marked out for his own, eager to do good.
Titus 1: 11-14 NEB

But although we speak as we do, we are convinced that you, my friends, are in the better case, and this makes for your salvation. For God would not be so unjust as to forget all that you did for love of his name, when you rendered service to his people, as you still do. But we long for every one of you to show the same eager concern, until your hope is finally realized. We want you not to become lazy, but to imitate those who, through faith and patience, are inheriting the promises.

When God make his promise to Abraham, he swore by himself, because he had no one greater to swear by: 'I vow that I will bless you abundantly and multiply you descendants.' Thus it was that Abraham, after patiently waiting, attained the promise. Men swear by a greater than themselves, and the oath provides a confirmation to end all dispute; and so God, desiring to show even more clearly to the heirs of his promise how unchanging was his purpose, guaranteed it by oath. Here, then, are two irrevocable acts in which

God could not possibly play us false, to give powerful encouragement to us, who have claimed his protection by grasping the hope set before us. That hope we hold. It is like an anchor for our lives, an anchor safe and sure. It enters in through the veil, where Jesus has entered on our behalf as forerunner, having become a high priest for ever in the succession of Melchizedek. **Hebrews 6: 9-20 NEB**

Praise be to the God and Father of our Lord Jesus Christ, who in his mercy gave us new birth into a living hope by the resurrection of Jesus Christ from the dead! The inheritance to which we are born is one that nothing can destroy or spoil or wither. It is kept for you in heaven, and you, because you put your faith in God, are under the protection of his power until salvation comes—the salvation which is even now in readiness and will be revealed at the end of time.

This is cause for great joy, even though now you smart for a little while, if need be, under trails of many kinds. Even gold passes through the assayer's fire, and more precious than perishable gold is faith which has stood the test. These trials come so that your faith may prove itself worthy of all praise, glory, and honor when Jesus Christ is revealed. You have not seen him, yet you love him; and trusting in him now without seeing him, you are transported with a joy too great for words, while you reap the harvest of your faith, that is, salvation for your souls. **I Peter 1: 3-9 NEB~**

You must therefore be like men stripped for action, perfectly self-controlled. Fix your hopes on the gift of grace which is to be yours when Jesus Christ is revealed. As obedient children, do not let your characters be shaped any longer by the desires you cherished in your days of ignorance. The One who called you is holy; like him, be holy in all your behavior, because Scripture says, 'You shall be holy, for I am holy.'

If you say 'our Father' to the One who judges every man impartially on the record of his deeds, you must stand in awe of him while you live out your time on earth. Well you know that it was no perishable stuff, like gold or silver, that bought your freedom from the empty folly of your traditional ways. The price was paid in precious blood, as it were of a lamb without mark or blemish—the blood of Christ. He was predestined before the foundation of the world, and in this last period of time he was made manifest for your sake. Through him you have come to trust in God who raised him from the dead and gave him glory, and so your faith and hope are fixed on God. **I Peter 1: 13-21 NEB**

LOVE

On one occasion an expert in the law stood up to test Jesus. "Teacher," he asked, "what must I do to inherit eternal life?" "What is written in the Law?" he replied. "How do you read it?" He answered: " 'Love the Lord your God with all your heart and with all your soul and with all your strength and with all your mind'; and, 'Love your neighbor as yourself.' " "You have answered correctly," Jesus replied. "Do this and you will live." But he wanted to justify himself, so he asked Jesus, "And who is my neighbor?" In reply Jesus said:

"A man was going down from Jerusalem to Jericho, when he fell into the hands of robbers. They stripped him of his clothes, beat him and went away, leaving him half dead. A priest happened to be going down the same road, and when he saw the man, he passed by on the other side. So too, a Levite, when he came to the place and saw him, passed by on the other side. But a Samaritan, as he traveled, came where the man was; and when he saw him, he took pity on him. He went to him and bandaged his wounds, pouring on oil and wine.

Then he put the man on his own donkey, took him to an inn and took care of him. The next day he took out two silver coins and gave them to the innkeeper. 'Look after him,' he said, 'and when I return, I will reimburse you for any extra expense you may have.' "Which of these three do you think was a neighbor to the man who fell into the hands of robbers?" The expert in the law replied, "The one who had mercy on him." Jesus told him, "Go and do likewise."
Luke 10: 25-37 NIV*

If you love me you will obey my commands; and I will ask the Father, and he will give you another to be your Advocate, who will be with you for ever—the Spirit of truth. The world cannot receive him, because the world neither sees nor knows him; but you know him, because he dwells with you and is in you. I will not leave you bereft; I am coming back to you. In a little while the world will see me no longer, but you will see me; because I live, you will live; then you will know that I am in my Father, and you in me and I in you. The man who has received my commands and obeys them—he it is who loves me; and he who loves me will be loved by my Father; and I will love him and disclose myself to him.'

Judas asked him—the other Judas, not Iscariot—'Lord, what can have happened, that you mean to disclose yourself to us alone and not to the world?' Jesus replied, 'Anyone who loves me will heed what I say; then my

Father will love him, and we will come to him and make our dwelling with him; but he who does not love me does not heed what I say. And the word you hear is not mine: it is the word of the Father who sent me. I have told you all this while I am still here with you; but your Advocate, the Holy Spirit whom the Father will send in my name, will teach you everything, and will call to mind all that I have told you.

'Peace is my parting gift to you, my own peace, such as the world cannot give. Set your troubled hearts at rest, and banish your fears. You heard me say, "I am going away, and coming back to you." If you loved me you would have been glad to hear that I was going to the Father; for the Father is greater than I. I have told you now, beforehand, so that when it happens you may have faith. I shall not talk much longer with you, for the Prince of this world approaches. He has no rights over me; but the world must be shown that I love the Father, and do exactly as he commands; so up, let us go forward!

John 14: 15-31 NEB

For at the very time when we were still powerless, then Christ died for the wicked. Even for a just man one of us would hardly die, though perhaps for a good man one might actually brave death; but Christ died for us while we were yet sinners, and that is God's own proof of his love towards us. And so, since we have now been justified by Christ's sacrificial death, we shall all the more certainly be saved through him from final retribution. For if, when we were God's enemies, we were reconciled to him through the death of his Son, much more, now that we are reconciled, shall we be saved by his life. But that is not all: we also exult in God through our Lord Jesus, through whom we now have been granted reconciliation. **Romans 5: 6-11 NEB**

Let no debt remain outstanding, except the continuing debt to love one another, for he who loves his fellowman has fulfilled the law. The commandments, "Do not commit adultery," "Do not murder," "Do not steal," "Do not covet," and whatever other commandment there may be, are summed up in this one rule: "Love your neighbor as yourself." Love does no harm to its neighbor. Therefore love is the fulfillment of the law. **Romans 13: 8-10 NIV**

I may be able to speak the languages of men and even of angels, but if I have no love, my speech is no more than a noisy gong or a clanging bell. I may have the gift of inspired preaching; I may have all knowledge and understand all secrets; I may have all the faith needed to move mountains—but if I have no love, I am nothing. I may give away everything I have, and even give up my body to be burned—but if I have no love, this does me no good.

Love is patient and kind; it is not jealous or conceited or proud; love is not ill-mannered or selfish or irritable;

love does not keep a record of wrongs; love is not happy with evil, but is happy with the truth. Love never gives up; and its faith, hope, and patience never fail.

Love is eternal. There are inspired messages, but they are temporary; there are gifts of speaking in strange tongues, but they will cease; there is knowledge, but it will pass. For our gifts of knowledge and of inspired messages are only partial; but when what is perfect comes, then what is partial will disappear.

When I was a child, my speech, feelings, and thinking were all those of a child; now that I am a man, I have no more use for childish ways. What we see now is like a dim image in a mirror; then we shall see face-to-face. What I know now is only partial; then it will be complete—as complete as God's knowledge of me. Meanwhile these three remain: faith, hope, and love; and the greatest of these is love.
I Corinthians 13: 1-13 GNB*

Be alert, stand firm in the faith, be courageous and strong. Everything you say and do should be done in love.
I Corinthians 16: 13-14 HOV

With this in mind, then, I kneel in prayer to the Father, from whom every family in heaven and on earth takes its name, that out of the treasures of his glory he may grant you strength and power through his Spirit in your inner being, that through faith Christ may dwell in your hearts in love. With deep roots and firm foundations, may you be strong to grasp, with all God's people, what is the breadth and length and height and depth of the love of Christ, and to know it, though it is beyond knowledge. So may you attain to fullness of being, the fullness of God himself.

Now to him who is able to do immeasurably more than all we can ask or conceive, by the power which is at work among us, to him be glory in the church and in Christ Jesus from generation to generation evermore! Amen.
Ephesians 3: 14-21 NEB~

This is how we know what love is: Christ gave his life for us. We too, then, ought to give our lives for our brothers! If a rich person sees his brother in need, yet closes his heart against his brother, how can he claim that he loves God? My children, our love should not be just words and talk; it must be true love, which shows itself in action.
I John 3: 16-18 GNB

Dear friends, if our hearts do not condemn us, we have confidence before God and receive from him anything we ask, because we obey his commands and do what pleases him. And this is his command: to believe in the name of his Son, Jesus Christ, and to love one another as he commanded us. Those who obey his commands live in him, and he in them. And this is how we know that he lives in us: We know it by the Spirit he gave us. **I John 3: 21-24 NIV**

Dear friends, let us love one another, because love comes from God. Whoever loves is child of God and knows God. Whoever does not love does not know God, for God is love. And God showed his love for us by sending his only Son into the world, so that we might have life through him. This is what love is: it is not that we have loved God, but that he loved us and sent his Son to be the means by which our sins are forgiven.

Dear friends, if this is how God loved us, then we should love one another. No one has ever seen God, but if we love one another, God lives in union with us, and his love is made perfect in us. We are sure that we live in union with God and that he lives in union with us, because he has given us his Spirit. And we have seen and tell others that the Father sent his Son to be the Savior of the world. If anyone declares that Jesus is the Son of God, he lives in union with God and God lives in union with him. And we ourselves know and believe the love which God has for us.

God is love, and whoever lives in love lives in union with God and God lives in union with him. Love is made perfect in us in order that we may have courage on the Judgment Day; and we will have it because our life in this world is the same as Christ's. There is no fear in love; perfect love drives out all fear. So then, love has not been made perfect in anyone who is afraid, because fear has to do with punishment.

We love because God first loved us. If someone says he loves God, but hates his brother, he is a liar. For he cannot love God, whom he has not seen, if he does not love is brother, whom he has seen. The command that Christ has given us is this: whoever loves God must love his brother also.

Whoever believes that Jesus is the Messiah is a child of God; and whoever loves a father loves his child also. This is how we know that we love God's children: it is by loving God and obeying his commands. For our love for God means that we obey his commands. And his commands are not too hard for us, because every child of God is able to defeat the world. And we win the victory over the world by means of our faith. Who can defeat the world? Only the person who believes that Jesus is the Son of God. **I John 4: 7- 5: 5 GNB+**

For God so loved the world that he gave his only Son, that whoever believes in him should not perish but have eternal life. **John 3:16 RSV***

REFERENCES

New Testament

Matthew 1:18-24 GNB-p. **11** // 3:1-3 RSV-p. **15** // 4:23-25 RSV-p. **21** // 5:1-12 RSV-p. **26***// 5:13-16 RSV-p. **26~** // 5:17-20 NIV-p. **79** // 5:23-24 NIV-p. **27** // 5:38-41 RSV-p. **27** // 5:43-46 RSV-p. **27+** // 6:1 RSV-p. **27** // 6:7-13 RSV-p. **28*** // 6:19-21 NIV-p. **28** // 6:25-33 RSV-p. **29** // 7:1-5 RSV-p. **29** // 7:7-8 NIV-p. **29** // 7:13-14 RSV-p. **29** // 7:21 NIV-p. **138** // 7:24-27 RSV-p. **30** // 9:35-38 RSV-p. **126** // 11:25-30 NEB-p. **185** // 13:1-9 RSV-p. **31** // 13:18-23 RSV-p. **31** // 13:44-50 RSV-p. **139** // 14:22-33 NEB-p. **205** // 18:1-8 GNB-p. **109** // 18:6-9 GNB-p. **206** // 18:15-17 GNB-p. **189** // 18:21-35 GNB-p. **173** // 19:13-15 NIV-p. **108** // 19:16-26 NTME-p. **115~** // 20:1-16 NTME-p. **86** // 20:25-28 NIV-p. **109** // 21:1-9 RSV-p. **34** // 21:28-32 NIV-p. **178** // 22:2-14 GNB-p. **89** // 24:36-44 GNB-p. **90** // 25:1-13 NIV-p. **89** // 25:14-30 GNB-p. **140** // 25:31-46 RSV-p. **91*** // 26:26-29 NIV-p. **37~** // 28:18-20 RSV-p. **129***

Old Testament

* "Top Ten" Passages

100 sheep… silver coins… two sons…

183 Psalm 23: 1-6
The Lord is my shepherd…

222 Luke 10: 25-37
Good Samaritan…Who is my neighbor?

225 I Corinthians 13: 1-13
The greatest of these is love…

228 John 3: 16
For God so loved the world…

+ "Plus Twenty" Passages

He humbled himself…

112 I Peter 2: 20-25
By his wounds you have been healed…

127 John 15: 1-17
I am the vine…you are the branches…

162 Psalm 100: 1-5
Serve the Lord with gladness…

168 Psalm 51: 1-17
Create in me a clean heart…

169 Romans 6: 1-11
Dead to sin and alive to God…

171 I John 1: 5-10
If we confess our sins…he will forgive…

175 Ephesians 2: 1-10
By grace you are saved…God's gift…

186 Romans 8: 31-39
If God is on our side… who is against us?

193 John 3: 1-17
Must be born over again…

195 John 10: 1-18
I am the door of the sheep...

212 Philippians 3: 6-11
Reckon as loss...power of his resurrection...

217 Romans 5: 1-5
Hope that will never disappoint....

218 Romans 8: 18-25
Universe waits with eager longing...

228 I John 4: 7-- 5: 5
We should love one another....

~ "FINAL TWENTY" PASSAGES

202 II Corinthians 9: 7-15
God loves…who gives cheerfully…

211 Galatians 2: 15-21
Justified through this faith…

213 Hebrews 11: 39-- 12: 2
Let us run with perseverance…

220 I Peter 1: 3-9
New birth into a living hope…

226 Ephesians 3: 14-21
Christ in your hearts…fullness of God…

Special Words — Occurrences

Action	23
Apostle	30
Authority	20
Baptize	24
Believe	100
Bless	60
Blood	27
Body	98
Bread	41
Brother	88
Call	109
Child	59
Chosen	18
Christ	279
Christian	16
Church	30
Confess	13
Covenant	14

Cross	**27**
Crucified	**17**
Dead	**55**
Disciple	**92**
Eat	**293**
Eternal Life	**22**
Evil	**62**
Faith	**166**
Father	**180**
Fire	**24**
Flesh	**33**
Follow	**53**
Food	**29**
Forgive	**44**
Free	**46**
Friend	**39**
Fruit	**28**
Gift	**47**
Glory	**60**
God	**755**
Good	**131**
Gospel	**47**
Grace	**66**
Happy	**14**
Heal	**24**
Heaven	**114**
Holy Spirit	**50**
Hope	**54**

Humble	**16**
Hungry	**17**
Jesus	**459**
Judgment	**30**
Justice	**23**
Kingdom	**62**
Law	**120**
Life	**136**
Light	**75**
Lord	**356**
Love	**204**
Money	**27**
Neighbor	**14**
Obey	**32**
Patience	**11**
Peace	**43**
Poor	**33**
Praise	**22**
Pray	**71**
Proclaim	**33**
Promise	**32**
Resurrection	**14**
Righteousness	**47**
Sacrifice	**16**
Salvation	**25**
Scripture	**47**
Seed	**18**
Servant	**60**

Serve	**51**
Sheep	**35**
Sign	**26**
Sin	**260**
Son	**273**
Suffering	**25**
Testimony	**19**
Thank	**42**
True	**33**
Truth	**70**
Trust	**27**
Union	**24**
Wash	**25**
Water	**51**
Win	**72**
Witness	**26**
Word	**100**
World	**119**
Worship	**27**

Sunday – March 12, 2006, 9:00 am

Last night I had "a dream," which had a significant impact on me. My son, Luther (it seemed to be him) and I had traveled to an unfamiliar city in a distant country. We parked our vehicle in a place we thought we could find. Off we went to see the sights; but it was a gloomy place with foreboding streets and threatening alleys. Many of the buildings were badly deteriorated and vacant. Wandering through this strange and lonely place we became separated. I was a bit concerned about whether I could find my way back to our vehicle, but I started on my way. Soon I realized I was lost, and as I peaked around one corner I was "overcome" by what seemed like a "bombed out" totally deteriorated area of the city. Most graphic was the fact that the whole scene was covered with countless people who had nothing! There was a massive hillside where seemingly all the people (sitting in large groups) had bundles of weeds covering them.

I was terrorized… and as I kept looking I realized that some order or "command to move out" had been given to these multitudes. And so they appeared to be moving—simply a vast vision of floating bundles of weeds—moving back up the long hillside and out of sight. I quickly turned away and began my walk back… now through crowded streets… in such distress at this scene that I was "beside myself". Finally, out of nowhere, I saw a blond pleasant looking woman coming toward me. As we met, I stopped her and asked if she was an American and/or Christian. Acknowledging she was, I told her that she was just the person I needed at that moment. My troubling experience "gushed out of me." I "broke down," putting my head on her shoulder and throwing my arms around her as I wept uncontrollably!

The dream quickly came to an end, and I woke up with unforgettable but clear memories.

The next morning, "it hit me" what I should have on my cover of "A Bible Story". Instead of "Fact or Fiction" surrounding my title (as my book, "Convicts Cheer Change"), I would run the word "Change." Repeated "change" would form a frame around the picture of a rainbow. "A Bible Story" would tell about love coming into the world to bring hope to needy people. Yes, Jesus inspires change that gives hope!

"A Bible Story" now takes on new urgency and a slightly different organization.

3/30/06 Being a Christian isn't just "changing", as good as that might be! Following Jesus is being in the process of doing a lot of divine "little things"—following in the footsteps of our Lord. My cover will reflect that truth.

www.ingramcontent.com/pod-product-compliance
Lightning Source LLC
LaVergne TN
LVHW041014150826
845672LV00001B/86

* 9 7 9 8 8 9 1 9 4 6 1 5 6 *